BOEING 777

Guy Norris & Mark Wagner

Worldwide Service

2071

Motorbooks International
Publishers & Wholesalers

First published in 1996 by Motorbooks International
Publishers & Wholesalers, 729 Prospect Avenue, PO Box 1,
Osceola, WI 54020 0001

The information in this book is true and complete to the best
of our knowledge. All recommendations are made without
any guarantee on the part of the author or Publisher, who also
disclaim any liability incurred in connection with the use of
this data or specific details

We recognize that some words, model names and
designations, for example, mentioned herein are the property
of the trademark holder. We use them for identification
purposes only. This is not an official publication
Motorbooks International books are also available at
discounts in bulk quantity for industrial or sales-promotional
use. For details write to Special Sales Manager at the
Publisher's address

Library of Congress Cataloging-in-Publication Data
Norris, Guy.
  Boeing 777 jetliners/Guy Norris, Mark Wagner.
    p. cm. — (Motorbooks International enthusiast color series)
Includes index.
ISBN 0-7603-0091-7 (pbk.: alk. paper)
1. Boeing 777 (Jet transport) I. Wagner, Mark. II. Title. III.
Series:Enthusiast color series.
TL686.B65N67   1996
629.133'349—dc20   95-50568

On the front cover: The 777 is Boeing's newest addition to its
family of airliners. *Boeing*
On the frontispiece: Kowloon Bay is visible in this wide-angle
view of an approach to Kai Tak International Airport's runway
31 in Hong Kong as presented by the CAE Maxiwide 2000
visual system. Note the overhead panel with larger lettering and
numbers than have been used in the past. The panel is fitted
with cool light emitting diode switches and lightplates.
A single switch controls the brightness of all the panels.
On the title page: With better-than-expected progress made on
the test program, WA003 took time off to make a lightning world
tour in April 1995. The aircraft is pictured here in London enroute
from Seattle to Cape Town and Johannesburg, South Africa.
On the back cover: The six-wheeled main undercarriage is
one of the most instantly recognizable features of the 777.

Printed in Hong Kong

CONTENTS

ACKNOWLEDGMENTS

Thanks to Mike Bair, Alan Mulally, Jeff Peace, and countless others at Boeing. Thanks particularly to Donna Mikov, Kirsti Dunn, Stephanie Mudgett, Barbara Murphy, Debbie Nomaguchi, and Doug Webb in Everett Communications. Also thanks to John Dern, Peter Sampson, Bill Fisher, Ken Hiebert, Greg Thon, Pat Woody, Steve Thieme, and Cindy Smith. Thanks to Gary Lesser and David Copeland of Boeing's *Airliner* magazine; also to Rick Kennedy of General Electric, Mark Sullivan of Pratt & Whitney, and Bob Stangerone, Martin Brodie, and Martin Johnson of Rolls Royce. Thanks to Jim Veihdeffer of Honeywell and Bill Reavis of AlliedSignal, both of Phoenix, Arizona. Thanks to Dennis Fernandez of British Airways, London, and Ron Allen of United Airlines, Seatac International Airport; also Eric Betten, Will Greenfield, Jennifer Bessler, and helicopter pilot Nicholas Ledington-Fischer. Thanks also to Tracey Deakin, John Dekker, Robert Freedman, Mark Hewish, Tim Mahon, and Dave Ruck. Thanks for inspiration from Sheila, Trevor, and Melanie, and to Lucy Bristow, Judy, and Tom for endless patience. And finally, a big thank you to Mike Haenggi, our editor at Motorbooks International.

INTRODUCTION

BOEING'S MAGNIFICENT SEVENTH

Boeing is very pleased with the 777, and rightly so. In less than five years it welded together an unprecedented international team of suppliers and airlines to help it make the biggest twin-engined jetliner in history. By 1998, when the first stretched 777-300 is due to be delivered, it will also be the longest jetliner ever built.

The 777 is vitally important to Boeing for two main reasons. First, it changed the way the company made jetliners right in the middle of the worst downturn in aerospace history. Boeing was forced into radical change because of the commitments it had made at the launch of the 777. The service-ready initiative at the heart of those commitments demanded levels of quality that only "Working Together" could hope to produce. As it turned out, the new-look Boeing not only produced a model development program, but also a blue-print for profit at a time when other large aerospace companies were merging to survive.

The 777's breakthroughs in technologies and advanced manufacturing and design techniques have been used so successfully that every project with Boeing involvement from the F-22 fighter to Space Station Alpha is following its lead. As company chairman and chief executive officer Frank Shrontz said at the handover of the first 777 to United Airlines in May 1995, "The 777 program set a new standard for the development of commercial aircraft, one that will influence the way airplanes are designed and built in our industry for many years to come."

Second, the 777 is vital to Boeing's future family plan. In creating the 777, the company now has a thoroughly modern jetliner that can be adapted to virtually every market sector need over 200 seats. The basic A-market 777-200 is being supplied for routes as varied as Denver to Honolulu and London to Washington, D.C. The next B-market version is to be capable of longer routes such as Los Angeles to London. At least two more variations are due by the end of the decade: a stretched 777-300, which will replace early model 747s on some routes, particularly in the Asia-Pacific area; and a shortened 777-100, which will fly ultra-long range routes like Dallas/Fort-Worth to Tokyo. Further off, when engine power is increased even more, the stretched twin will have the "legs" to fly 747-400 routes.

The end result is a family of jetliners unparalleled in the industry, ranging from the diminutive 737-600 at one end of the scale to the 777-300 and 747-400 at the other. By late 1995, the 777 order book had exceeded 200, and the certainty of more versions guarantees that this is sure to climb. Sales of the 777 will play a big part in helping the total Boeing order book break the incredible 9,000 jetliner mark (more than all other jetliner producers in the world combined) in the coming years.

This book, lavishly illustrated with the most up-to-date photographs of the aircraft and production line, traces the development of the new jetliner. It also explains why the 777 looks like it does and what shaped the design process. The 777 is also reviewed from top to bottom, inside and out, with every major system described and explained.

With at least $4 billion of Boeing investment, and up to another $2 billion of suppliers' money behind it, the 777 is likely to be the last all-new widebody jetliner produced this century by either Boeing or any other airframer. If this is indeed the case, the 777 is a fitting culmination to the end of the first century of manned flight and an impressive standard to set for the start of the next.

Guy Norris
November 1995

CHAPTER 1

GENESIS

During the winter of 1986 Boeing's products were selling well. The 737, newly revitalized with the more modern CFM56 powerplant, was heading for the record books. New designs to dramatically upgrade the 747 were underway with the year-old -400 program. Even the slow-selling 757 and 767 lines had started to pick up as the new market for medium and long range twins began to emerge.

In the middle of all this, Boeing saw the first glimmer of a potentially huge new market niche. The new long range success of the 767 prompted Boeing to begin looking at a new product to fit between the 767-300 and 747. The new aircraft was aimed at a juicy target—a replacement for hundreds of McDonnell Douglas DC-10s and Lockheed L-1011s that plied the transcontinental US trunk routes and other sectors around the world. At first, it seemed that a relatively straightforward stretch of the 767, to carry around 300, would do the job. But then things began to change.

Cathay Pacific had a major influence on the cabin width, strongly pushing for 747-like dimensions.

Customer satisfaction is the bottom line. Most of the airlines wanted something wider than the 767 with a new interior and the very latest in in-flight entertainment systems. What you see is what you get in this first-class cabin of a United 777. Note the large overhead bin, sculpted side panels, and seat-mounted video screen.

Developing a replacement for the popular McDonnell Douglas DC-10 was one of the major drivers of the early 767-X program. A DC-10 is seen symbolically climbing into the distant sunset behind this newly delivered United 777 on a summer evening in 1995.

United launched the 777 with orders for 34, and options for an additional 34.

The new influence was the airlines themselves. Up until the 777, the airlines had not played much of a direct role in shaping the basic design details of any Boeing jetliner. However, by the time Boeing began its search for a 767 follow-on, the competition for the same market niche was already springing up. McDonnell Douglas was well on with development of the MD-11, a virtually new derivative of the DC-10, while Airbus was working on the A330 and A340, a pair of new-technology medium/long range widebodies. Boeing was therefore coming from behind and recognized that it needed direction from the market.

As a result, Boeing began asking the carriers what they wanted and got unexpected answers. By 1988, after extensive talks with several airlines, it became obvious that a derivative of the 767 was not the favored option. The market told Boeing that it needed a totally new airplane. Heeding the wishes of the airlines, Boeing decided to stick with its radical new policy. From then on, the 767-X, as the project was known, was

Artist's impressions of early 767-X configurations, both versions of which were direct developments of the basic 767 airframe. *Boeing*

firmly "market driven" with airlines advising Boeing on the new design every step of the way.

Over in Chicago that same year, United Airlines began doing some calculations. It realized that its reliable old/workhorse, the DC-10 (or Diesel 10 as it is affectionately known by the airline), would be 25 years old by 1996. Therefore, within two years it started a fleet replacement program that would soon lead to the birth of the 777.

By December 1989, the pressure was on Boeing to start firming things up. Its marketers told them that the omens were good; and on December 8, the company's board of directors authorized Boeing Commercial Airplane Group to issue firm offers to airlines on the 767-X. The New Airplane Division was established in Renton by the end of the year with Phil Condit, a rising star at Boeing, named as vice president and general manager.

The next year was even busier for Boeing. On a cold January day back in Seattle, Boeing held the first formal meeting of its "Working Together" airlines. These had been gathered to help establish the basic configuration of the 767-X and included eight of the world's leading airlines—All Nippon Airways, American Airlines, British Airways, Cathay Pacific Airways, Delta Air Lines, Japan Airlines, Qantas Airways, and United Airlines. At the first meeting, each airline was given a 23-page questionnaire about what it wanted to see on the new airplane.

Until this time the design inputs had been confused. Even the external shape was still in debate. Some wanted a family of airliners like the 737 concept, others preferred a twin-engined design that would carry 25 percent more than the L-1011, seating up to 10 abreast in economy class, and having the same advanced flight deck as the 747-400, which had just been launched.

Although Boeing lagged behind the competition, the black cloud had a silver lining. The Airbus and McDonnell Douglas aircraft were committed to production, so Boeing could design the 767-X to be a bit bigger, with more range, and a new cross-section. It was turning the tables on Douglas, which 30 years earlier had designed the "paper" DC-8 to be slightly bigger and faster than the 707.

Boeing already knew that the 767 wing was not large enough to base the new aircraft around, and had already started looking at something new. It had no problems confirming that a twin was the best solution. Using baseline fuel consumption and maintenance costs, a four-engined design was estimated to be 20 to 30 percent higher in costs, while a twin with new engines was roughly 10 percent lower. The disadvantage of the twin was that it needed a new engine more powerful than any then flying. On the other hand, the four-engined version would have also required the development of a brand new 40,000 pound (178kN) thrust engine. A trijet design was considered and rejected because of the cost and complexity of the large "banjo (shaped) fitting" in the tail.

At one stage, Boeing even studied an ugly-looking hybrid which simply mated the 767 with half of a 757 riding piggy-back on top of the aft fuselage. The "hunchback of Mukilteo," as the misfit was nicknamed after a local area, was thankfully rejected because it could not carry enough cargo, but mainly because it just didn't look right!

By March 1990, the "Working Together" groups produced a basic configuration for the 767-X. Thanks mainly to Cathay Pacific's insistence, the new twin's cabin cross-section was within inches of the 747 and could carry 325 passengers in three classes. Other airlines, including United, told Boeing the new airplane should have "fly-by-wire," or electrically signaled controls and a 747-400-style "glass" cockpit. Other suggestions were that it should have a flexible interior; gate commonality with the DC-10; a big built-in, self-test capability; and 10 percent better dollars per aircraft seat-mile costs than the A330 or MD-11. Crucially, United also told Boeing that the 777 should, if possible, have ETOPS (extended-range twin operations) from day one. Until this point, every new airliner had to earn the right to fly up to three hours away from a suitable diversionary airport by flying thousands of trouble-free hours in service.

The new aircraft would have a range of 4,600 miles (7,406km) in its initial version, but Boeing was beginning to see that the design had far greater potential. With some development, the new 767-X could be capable of greater ranges and payloads. In

All Nippon Airways helped influence the final size of the -200 by requesting a slightly longer basic model.

short, the twin would be the start of an entirely new family which could not only replace L-1011s and DC-10s, but eventually even its own 747.

Meanwhile United's ambitious new widebody program was becoming the focus for Boeing's efforts. The airline was looking at three different cabin capacities (250, 350, and 450 passengers) and three distinct markets (Pacific, Atlantic, and domestic). Its real target, however, was a DC-10 replacement to fly two very different types of routes, Chicago to Hawaii and Chicago to Europe. In addition, the airline also wanted an aircraft able to fly non-stop from 5,000 foot-high Denver airport on a hot day, to Hawaii. The flight to Hawaii was the "hidden" factor. Any manufacturer committing to this requirement would need to achieve ETOPS from day one, something never-before attempted.

After months of presentations, United's final selection took place over an exhaustive 70-hour session in Chicago between October 12 and 14, 1990. Airbus, Boeing, and McDonnell Douglas were there, as were General Electric, Pratt & Whitney, and Rolls-Royce. Between the A330, 777-200, MD-11, GE90, GECF6, PW4084, PW4164, Trent 700, and Trent 800, United was faced with 33 different engine-airframe combinations. It was a "matrix migraine," said Gordon McKinzie, United's 777 program manager.

Finally, on the afternoon of Saturday, October 14, United announced that it had signed a letter of intent for 34 Pratt & Whitney-powered 777s, with 34 options potentially worth billions of dollars. The agreement was sealed with a hand-written pledge between the two companies. It read:

In order to launch on-time a truly great airplane we have a responsibility to work together to design, produce, and introduce an airplane that exceeds the expectations of flight crews, cabin crews, and maintenance and support teams and ultimately our passengers and shippers.

From day one:
• Best dispatch reliability in the industry
• Greatest customer appeal in the industry
• User friendly and everything works

The document was signed by United's Executive Vice President, Operations, Jim Guyette; Phil Condit, Vice President of the New Airplane Division; and Dick Albrecht, Executive Vice President of Sales at Boeing.

The paper pledge could have been carved in stone, such was its profound impression on Boeing, the suppliers, airlines, and the 777 itself. There were two main reasons why United pushed the idea of "Working Together" with Boeing. First, the painful memories of introducing the 747-400 were still fresh in its collective memory. "It was tough for us," said McKinzie. "We had sold seats that we had to give up for six months because the plane just wasn't ready. The program was basically underscoped in terms of

complexity, and Boeing was badly bruised by the experience. It was a very important 'lesson learned.'"

Second, "...we thought we had some 'tribal knowledge and experience' we thought we could bring to the program. So we decided to call Boeing and tell them that we wanted in on the airplane from the start. We virtually infiltrated the Boeing design process," he said.

Two weeks after United's order was announced, the Boeing board gave its formal approval to the launch of the 777. At the same time, the division was renamed the 777 Division of Boeing Commercial Airplane Group. Its leader, Phil Condit, was later to become Boeing President and the division was to be headed by Alan Mulally who took over in 1992. Mulally, an astronautical engineer by training with a master's degree in management from the Massachusetts Institute of Technology, together with engineering experience on virtually every Boeing jetliner, was to become the energetic driver at the center of the entire 777 effort.

A month after the agreement was signed, United's 777 development team arrived in Seattle and moved inside "Fortress" Boeing. The real task of building the 777 had begun.

The first complete aircraft, N7771, cruises high over the coast of California during the intensive flight test program. *Boeing*

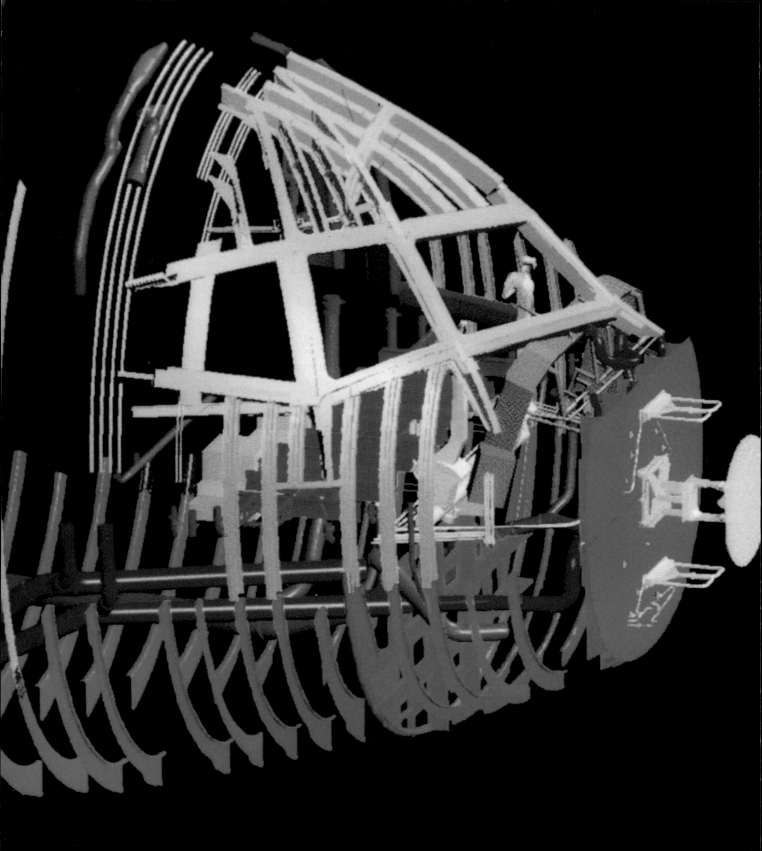

CHAPTER 2

JOURNEY INTO CYBERSPACE

Boeing basically needed to reinvent itself to make the 777. It quickly realized that the promise of creating a "service ready" design from day one could not be achieved by the "old" Boeing, and enormous structural and cultural changes were going to have to be made.

"Working Together" with United and the other airlines was one way, but it was not only cultural changes that were needed. Extra space was required to make the new airliner. Boeing spent nearly $1.5 billion doubling the size of its Everett facility to provide more area for two 777 assembly lines alongside the 747 and 767 production lines. To make the new jetliner more efficiently, and to cut out the high costs of rework, it also took the bold step of introducing a computer-based three-dimensional design system-called CATIA (explained later in this chapter). Another ground-breaking initiative was the creation of

Digital pre-assembly drastically cut the number of interferences that often plagued previous jetliners in the early-design stages. To confirm its faith in CATIA, Boeing made a mock-up of the nose area, or Section 41, pictured in digital format above. *Boeing*

Boeing pumped around $1.5 billion into an expansion of the Everett site to accommodate the 777. Some 275,000 cubic yards of concrete were poured to form the floor of the site, enough to make 44 miles (72km) of four-lane freeway. The huge site also required 85,000 tons of steel, or virtually twice the amount needed to erect the Empire State Building in New York. The 777 extension includes the buildings to the far right and the new paint hangar closest to them.

Anxious moments as the first 777 is put together. Workers breathed a sigh of relief as the fuselage joined together more smoothly than any previous Boeing jetliner. *Boeing*

a huge, $370 million laboratory in which every part of the aircraft would be thoroughly tested and simulated before the real 777 even flew.

Working Together

In November 1990, a small 777 development team from United moved into Boeing. This was the first real evidence of "Working Together" and the enormous changes that were to follow. They were soon followed by similar teams from All Nippon Airways, British Airways, and Japan Airlines. Unlike previous programs like the 747, these airline offices were not in "airline row" at the delivery center, but were right in the heart of Boeing's design engineering offices.

At first, Boeing engineers found it difficult to adjust to the new setup, as did the various airline representatives. In the past, the relationship between the manufacturer and its customers had often been confrontational. Now both sides were forced to overcome natural prejudices and be trusting and honest with each other. In the end, the results were better than anyone predicted. Out of about 1,500 design issues dealt with by the teams, some 300 were new design directions that Boeing would not otherwise have taken.

Many of the items were incredibly small but vitally important to improving the reliability and maintainability of the 777. Boeing willingly accepted the input of the airlines realizing that although it was good at making aircraft, it had no experience operating them. The inputs early in the 777 development enabled Boeing to alter the design before tooling was made, keeping the cost down. Many of the changes also avoided the potential cost of retrofits to correct problems that might only have come to light in flight test, or even in service.

"Working Together" with British Airways, for example, produced more than 100 changes to the basic aircraft specification. These included the

The front right spar for the wing of the 31st 777, destined for Cathay Pacific, takes shape. Extensive use of automated machine tools, like this one, have helped improve efficiency and quality on the production line.

adoption of radial-ply tires for the nose-gear, making the 777 the first US commercial jet to be certified with radial-ply as standard. Others included a "maintenance friendly" on-board engine vibration system, a device that stores all the loadable software, and a revised galley design at the rear of the aircraft that provides room for four extra seats.

United Airlines also generated a series of significant changes. These included a revised trailing-edge flap design that can be disassembled into two parts so that it fits in an autoclave for repair. Boeing wanted to make the 43-foot-long (13.1m) composite structure in one piece, but United won the argument. Another was the replacement of one long leading-edge access panel with lots of small ones so that mechanics would not need to remove scores of screws to find one problem.

Other areas of influence included larger push buttons on access panels. These were made bigger so that mechanics wearing gloves on a freezing day at Chicago O'Hare could activate them. United also influenced the design to include a "towbarless" tractor nose-gear design; the use of nickel- instead of silver-plated fuel-tank wiring to prevent corrosion; and the use of passenger reading lights that could be replaced by flight attendants. All Nippon Airways and United together compromised on a wing fueling point that Boeing had originally designed at a higher location than on the 747. An unusual concern from one airline was that the normal lavatory seat used on the aircraft would slam down and wake up business and first class passengers. A specially designed "no-slam-can" was therefore used in the 777!

Design Build Teams

Teaming is a big word at Boeing thanks to the 777 experience. At one point almost 240 design build teams (DBTs) were working on the aircraft, some of which had up to 40 members. The use of DBTs changed the traditional methods of construction at Boeing where the design of individual sections or systems on the aircraft would be completed by small groups of specialists before being "thrown over the wall" to the next group. Under this system, if something was wrong with the design to start with, the effects of this would be amplified downstream, adding to changes in drawings and tooling, and ultimately raising costs.

DBTs brought together customers and suppliers involved in a particular area of the airplane. This created a forum in which everybody's voice was heard and the design altered accordingly. Sometimes designs took longer to be finalized as a result, but the overall benefits were startling, and DBTs will form the basis for virtually every Boeing program in the future.

Another benefit of DBTs was that each organization involved in the team was able to coordinate its work schedule to slot into the time frame of the others. This "concurrent" engineering led to major time saving, less change, error, and rework. A typical DBT working on part of the fuselage included people from planning, tooling, producibility, the factory, material, and the various systems that would run through that particular part. In the past, many of these groups would have only had the chance to work their wires, hydraulic lines, and brackets into the fuselage section after it been designed by the structures group. This resulted in a lot of change to the "final" design. By working together, the entire unit was designed to accommodate the needs of every group simultaneously.

A Gemcor riveting machine inserts seven fasteners per minute. In all, the four-panel wing set requires some 68,000 fasteners.

CATIA

Before the 777 was launched, Boeing's internal research showed that huge manufacturing costs could be saved if parts fitted together better the first time, and if less expensive "rework" was needed to complete the structure. It was decided that Boeing should take the plunge and produce the new twinjet entirely on computer to assure the benefits it was looking for.

The 777 therefore became the first 100 percent paperless Boeing jetliner. It was designed using the IBM/Dassault digital design system called CATIA (Computer-Aided Three-dimensional Interactive Applications).

Using this method, all the designs are created with three-dimensional solid images. When all the bits are put together on the screen the system can detect if the fit is not perfect and if some parts, such as ducts and wires, interfere with each other. Boeing was still not totally convinced that CATIA was workable so it built a mock-up of the complicated nose (section 41), to verify the system. It was so successful that plans for a similar verification on a fuselage part (section 43) were dropped. For the first time on any of its commercial jetliners, Boeing did not build a conventional engineering mock-up.

CATIA was even able to check if humans could crawl in and out of the tight spaces inside areas like the avionics bay. To accomplish this, a computer-generated human model, variously known as CATIA-man, or Robocop, was moved around every nook and cranny of the cyberspace 777.

Unlike previous Boeing jetliners, the 777 moves down the final part of the assembly line without engines. This reflects the change to "just-in-time" manufacturing, which cuts down on unnecessary and hugely expensive inventory until it is really needed. This particular 777 was destined for Cathay Pacific and was the second to be powered by the Rolls-Royce Trent.

Although CATIA was cumbersome and expensive to operate at first, the improvements in quality have more than paid back Boeing's investment. After lasers aligned and leveled all the major sections of the fuselage and wings of the first 777, the port wingtip of the completed aircraft was a mere 0.001 inch out of alignment. The fuselage was out of alignment by a scant 0.023 inch. At peak stages of the initial 777-200 design, more than 2,200 CATIA workstations were networked into a cluster of eight IBM 3090-600J mainframe computers—the largest cluster in the world. Upgraded CATIA software was brought into the system for use on the design of the 777-200 B-market, 777-300 Stretch, and 777-100 Shrink.

The movement of the rudder was carefully tested and calibrated in the "Iron Bird" flight-control test rig within the integrated aircraft systems lab. A large marker provides a visual reference for the movement of the fin in degrees.

The benefits of CATIA also spread out beyond the Boeing design offices to component suppliers around the world which use the same database for concurrent development of other parts. This mainly includes three Japanese companies: Mitsubishi, Kawasaki, and Fuji Heavy Industries, which together form the Japan Aircraft Development Corporation and take a 20 percent share of the 777. The group builds most of the fuselage panels and doors, wing center section, wing-to-body fairing, and wing in-spar ribs. Other major overseas suppliers include Alenia of Italy, which supplies outboard wing flaps and the radome; Embraer of Brazil, which makes part of the wingtip and flap support; Aerospace

Technologies of Australia, which is making the all-composite rudder; and fellow Australian company Hawker de Havilland, which makes the elevators. The nose gear doors are also made outside of the United States by Short Brothers of Northern Ireland and Singapore Aerospace.

Significant US suppliers of structural parts include Boeing's other major site in Wichita, Kansas; Northrop Grumman; Rockwell; and Kaman Aerospace. Smaller suppliers include California-based Astech/MCI and Colorado-based Explosive Fabricators.

Digital data from CATIA is also fed to automated manufacturing machines that have been built into the massive new factory space created for the 777. Boeing added the world's largest extension, a 32 acre, six-story high structure, to what was already the world's biggest building. The total area, now covering around 64 acres, produces the 767-200, 200ER, 767-300, 300ER and -300F, 747-400 and -400F, and 777-200. With a maximum capacity for up to seven 777s a month, the line will also assemble the stretched 777-300, and possibly the short body -100 if built. Pride-of-place in the factory is taken by the automated wing spar assembly machine. This fixes thousands of bolts and rivets to the aircraft's 105 foot (32m) wing spar and effectively stretches it by around 0.5 inch as it does so.

"Build-Test-Fix"

Second only to Boeing's huge investment in the enlarged factory was its $370 million development of a new Integrated Aircraft Systems Laboratory (IASL). This unique facility was built near Boeing Field and contains shops and labs that replicate the actual aircraft. The investment continues to be well used. With the successful launch of the 777-200 A-market, the lab was next turned onto the heavier B-market 777-200, the 777-300, and the next generation of 737 narrowbody twinjets, the -600/700 and -800.

The IASL does such a convincing job of replicating the 777 that it has been called "aircraft zero," "777 No. 0," and "the skinless aircraft" by Boeing employees. By developing the IASL, Boeing was able to "smoke out" problems with individual com-

The dismembered remains of the static test airframe sit forlornly behind the Everett factory with other carcasses. The static airframe was the second 777 built, and was made to demonstrate that the structure was capable of withstanding the highest possible loading under the most extreme flight or ground conditions ever likely to be experienced in the life of the 777 fleet. More than 4,300 strain gauges were attached to the airframe, which was finally dismantled in 1995 after the wing was tested to destruction in January that year. Remains of the wing are seen to the left. A former Japan Airlines 747SR fuselage, used for fatigue research, stands behind the 777.

Right
A panorama of the "Iron Bird" reveals the main control and power cables linking the tail assembly (left) and the left wing (right). The rig is controlled by a dedicated cockpit simulator and tests the interfaces between systems as well as the interplay of the fly-by-wire system with the autopilot and flight director.

Left
The distinctive six-wheeled main undercarriage bogie was rigorously tested in the "Iron Bird," where it was put through 40,000 simulated takeoffs and landings.

The fourth 777 off the line was also destined never to fly, but was put through two lifetimes of simulated operation as the fatigue test airframe. It started "flying" in January 1995, and by July of that year had already amassed the equivalent of 25,000 cycles. The test was set to finish in late-1996 and was designed to unearth any weaknesses in the structure that would show up later in service. Some parts, like the inboard flap and engine strut, are tested separately. The horizontal stabilizer is also tested in its own rig near the nose of the 777. To simulate cabin pressure at altitude, the fuselage is pumped up with air to 8.6psi (0.6 bar) in less than 15 seconds during each "flight." The 200 fuselage has a pressurized volume of 46,000 cubic feet (1,624 cubic meters)

One hundred hydraulic actuators pump and pummel the airframe over each flight cycle, which lasts an average of four minutes. These continue 24 hours a day and simulate everything from ground handling and taxi, to takeoff, cruise, descent, depressurization, and even bad turbulence. More than 1,000 strain gauges were initially attached to the airframe.

Completion work continues well after painting. Here All Nippon Airways' first 777 receives undivided attention on the Everett ramp.

ponents and complete systems long before flight testing took place. This "build-test-fix" philosophy enabled the company to save both time and money during the already compressed flight test program. Within its 518,000sq ft of floor space, the lab tested 57 major 777 systems, 3,500 line-replaceable units (pieces of equipment that can be removed from the aircraft relatively simply during maintenance), and 20,000 additional parts supplied by 241 companies in the United States and 11 overseas nations.

Equipment arrived in the lab and was quickly checked by one of up to 70 dedicated IASL stand-alone test stations. Once it passed this hurdle, the part was passed on to one of eight subsystem integration test facilities where it was placed into its relevant system. These included the landing gear, cabin management system, electrical power generation system, brakes, leading edge/trailing edge, electronic engine controls, autopilot/flight director, and the aircraft information management system (AIMS).

The landing gear test lab, for example, contained full-scale nose and main landing gear legs. These were wired-up, or fully instrumented, to record every reaction to the stresses and strains imposed on them. They were subjected to simulated airspeeds of up to 270 knots (311mph or 500km/h) by forcing hydraulic rams against them. The lab was later used to take the gear through 40,000 simulated takeoffs and landings as part of the enormous fatigue test program.

Fatigue testing on a complete 777 airframe was undertaken in the traditional way. Beginning in spring 1994, the fatigue-test 777 began seven months of pressurization and loading to simulate more than two entire design lifetimes. Another static-test airframe, which began evaluation in June 1994, was finally tested to destruction on January 14 the following year. The wings were pulled up 24 feet (7.3m) above their normal position until they broke at more than one and a half times the loads experienced during the most extreme flight conditions.

Three more "super labs" lay beyond the subsystem integration test facilities. These were known as the major integration test facilities which covered the test of all the aircraft's systems, its cockpit, and fight controls. The system integration lab (SIL) checked the function and interoperability of the electrical, avionics, and sensor systems. The entire SIL was taken for a "flight" several times a day during which every part of the 777 in the lab was made to behave as if it was over Seattle at 30,000 feet. At its peak, the SIL was "flying" around 400 times per month. A dedicated test-aircraft, on the other hand, would be hard pressed to fly even one quarter of this time in real life.

The second major lab was a cockpit that was used to sort out where instruments and displays would be located. It also evaluated the complex interplay between major systems such as the autopilot, AIMS, and flight director. The third, and most unusual looking lab was the flight controls test rig, or "Iron Bird" as it was more frequently called. This was used to validate the fly-by-wire (FBW) flight control system by moving the aircraft's flight feathers—an aileron, rudder, elevator, and a set of spoilers.

An impressive array of computers support the IASL. The "big three" labs are plugged into a bank of 43 Harris Night Hawk computers. These have multiple parallel processors and run simulations so fast that they actually occur more quickly than a real-time event. The less demanding simulations are run on Concurrent computers.

A British Airways 777 stands poised to receive its livery inside the dedicated paint hangar. This aircraft, registered G-ZZZE, was destined to be named Sir John Alcock/Sir Arthur Whitten Brown in honor of the first aviators to fly nonstop across the North Atlantic.

Another highly unusual lab was the PCEL or Passenger Cabin Engineering Lab. This was built at Everett with more than 100 seats and used to test everything that would appear in the cabin. The most complicated cabin system, and the biggest integration challenge, was the inflight entertainment system. Compared to previous aircraft, the 777's inflight entertainment system is the most complex system of its kind ever developed and with an estimated 250,000 lines of dedicated software code, is as sophisticated as the entire avionics systems of most commercial aircraft that were built in the late 1980s.

Each seat in the new aircraft has the equivalent capability of a 386-laptop computer with up to 12 video channels and 48 audio channels available to the passenger. In addition, each seat has a hand-held phone that doubles as a game controller, credit/phone card reader, and modem link. A typical installation, as supplied by GEC Marconi or Matsushita, has up to 2,000 individual units and can weigh almost 9,000 pounds (2,745kg).

Testing went at an impressive rate and problems were found in many systems that would have cropped up in flight test and caused substantial delays. Yet, despite the most thorough testing in the history of aviation, Boeing was still in for a few surprises when the real airplane finally took to the air to begin the flight test program in June 1994.

CHAPTER 3

INSIDE THE 777

Boeing took a "clean sheet" approach to the 777. By the time it began design work on the 767-X project in the late 1980s, a decade had passed since the launch of the last pair of all-new Boeings, the 757 and the 767. A lot of new technology had become commercially practical in that time, such as advanced composite materials, and much of it was to be applied to the new design.

By far the largest design difference visible from the outside is the aircraft's round cross-section. This distinguishes it from any previous Boeing jetliner. Viewed nose-on, the 777 is perfectly circular. Every one of its predecessors is basically ovoid—or dou-

Right
The 777 is the first Boeing jetliner to be completely circular in cross-section.

Left
The impressive width of the cabin is already evident in this tunnel-like view of the rear fuselage before the final body is joined. Note the rear pressure bulkhead and the toughened (graphite) carbon composite floor beams running across the fuselage.

The all-composite rudder is made out of the same basic carbon (graphite) material used to make large parts of the engine cowlings, flaps, spoilers, and the main- and nose-undercarriage doors.

ble bubble—with the cross-section made up of two circular arcs of different radii. The larger circle is above and faired into the lower to form a smooth contoured ellipse.

Boeing's two previous widebody jets, the 747 and the 767, had emerged with different cross-sections for many reasons, mostly related to cargo space. The 21.3 foot (6.5m) wide 747 was built around the space requirement of cargo containers on the main deck. When the 747 was being designed in the late 1960s, the launch customer Pan Am was convinced that a new generation of supersonic transports would soon relegate the subsonic jets to cargo duties.

Despite appearing like a PR gimmick, the liveried rudders of these 777s are painted before the rest of the airframe so that they will be properly balanced. The delicate adjustment of the rudder can be affected by the weight of the paint applied to each side of the rudder itself.

The graceful lines of the 777's advanced aerodynamic wing are displayed to good effect in this air-to-air shot of a United test aircraft. The "inverse camber" is clearly visible in the curved underside of the wing at the trailing edge. *Boeing*

The full sweep of the slender-looking wing is captured on this engineless All Nippon Airways aircraft. Note the full-span leading-edge slats and simple single-slotted trailing-edge flaps.

The 767 on the other hand, was contoured around a single large cargo container on the main deck and a longitudinal lower lobe pallet measuring 8 feet (2.4m) by 10.4 feet (3.1m). In the end, most 767s ended up carrying two LD-2 containers on the lower deck, and seven abreast economy seating on the main deck; though the 767-300F Freighter was finally ordered and flying by 1995. The 767 cross-section philosophy resulted in a width of 16.5 feet (5.0m).

The 777 sits right between the two with a fuselage width of 20.3 feet (6.20m). The resulting cross-section fits perfectly around two LD-3s, the most common under-floor cargo container in the air today. It also makes it 22 inches (53.9cm) externally wider than the competition, allowing Boeing to provide one extra seat per row than the A330/340. The biggest benefit to the airlines is expected to be the aircraft's enormous below-deck cargo capability, which is even more than a 747-400 in terms of weight but not volume. Boeing is so sure that the 777 will eventually be offered as a Combi (freight/passenger) or an all-freight aircraft in the future that a huge cargo door has already been designed. The door is now available as an option and adds about 992 pounds (450kg) to the overall weight.

A circular cross-section also brings other benefits. It is easier to build and lighter because no fairings are needed to smooth out the differences between the different radii of the upper and lower sections. It is also structurally simpler and stronger, and less prone to fatigue. The sheer size of the new aircraft and the expected stresses and strains that it will need to endure in its long-planned life led Boeing to use several new high-strength materials.

A new aluminum alloy from Alcoa called 2XXX is used for the fuselage skin. It has a higher fracture toughness than a standard aircraft aluminum called 2024, which has been used for fuselages in the past. A large dome-shaped aft pressure bulkhead, which maintains the back end of the 777's pressure vessel, is also made out of 2XXX.

Another type of alloy, 7150, is used for the fuselage stringers—parts of the airframe structure that run lengthwise through the frames to support the skin. Each stringer is like a "Z" in cross-section instead of the normal "U" or "I." This shape stops water from damming up when it condenses and runs down the skin inside the fuselage, and therefore slows down the chances of any corrosion. As the creation of moisture can be a big corrosion issue in wide-bodied aircraft, Boeing has gone one step further to prevent water spreading. Support struts which hold the ceiling to the skin of the roof are enclosed in giant sponges that soak up water as it drips down.

Corrosion is the number-one enemy of older aircraft. And Boeing has gone to enormous lengths to cut down the chances of it being a problem in other traditionally troubled areas: the galley, toilets, and underneath seats where drinks are often spilled. The airlines expressed the wish for "flexible zones" where toilets and galleys could be quickly moved in or out. This instant replumbing capability enables the airline to respond to changing passenger demand and means the 777 can be reconfigured to seat more economy or business class passengers in hours rather than days. Although this was good for the airlines, it gave Boeing a headache because it meant more areas of the floor had to be prepared with extra anti-corrosion treatments.

Once Boeing and its airline advisory group had hammered out exactly where and how large the flex zones were to be, the company put corrosion-resistant titanium seat-racks in those areas. Transverse support beams supporting the tracks are made from composites of carbon fiber and toughened resins. The floor panels attached to this structure are also made out of composites. This is better for corrosion resistance and is lighter than aluminum.

In all, composite materials make up around 9 percent of the 777, some three times as much as any previous Boeing jetliner. Most of it is used in the tail area, where, for the first time on any Boeing airliner, composite material is used for primary, or main, structure. The main torque box of the vertical stabilizer, for example, is a carbon-fiber reinforced unit, built up from the front and rear spars and ribs. Carbon-fiber reinforced composites also make up the panels covering the tail. Only one of the three spars

The "gull-winged" effect is pronounced in this wide-angle view from the tail.

in the tail is made from aluminum, the other two being carbon-fiber reinforced plastic.

Even the rudder is made from carbon-fiber-epoxy sandwich panels attached to two composite spars and ribs. Composites are also used for moving wing trailing edge surfaces and spoiler panels, wing fixed leading edges, engine nacelles, wing root fairings, and main landing gear doors. Altogether, Boeing saved 2,600 pounds (1,180kg) of equivalent structural weight by using composites. The company also saved a hefty 3,200 pounds (1,450kg) by using advanced alloys.

The Wing

The 777 wing is huge by any standards. It spans almost 200 feet (61m) and has an area of 4,628 square feet (430m sq). It is also distinctively angled-up to provide ground clearance for the enormous engines and is "gulled" (gull-winged) near the fuselage to provide a large enough housing for the tall undercarriage.

Boeing has a tradition of big wings going back to the days of the B-29 bomber. With the jet age this continued with aircraft such as the B-52 and 707 and eventually the 747, which eclipsed everything that had flown before. The wings of the latest 747 version, the -400, are extended even further with winglets to produce a span of 211 feet (64.3m). The winglets, canted 22 degrees outward and swept by 60 degrees, improve aerodynamic efficiency by de-

creasing drag and increase the -400 range by 3 percent. When the aircraft is fully loaded with fuel on the ground, the wings hang slightly lower with the extra weight and the winglets bend further outwards, actually increasing the span a few feet!

Using new aerodynamic analysis techniques, Boeing developed special airfoil designs in the 1970s which it used for the first time on the 757 and 767. Unlike the sharply swept 747 wing, which has a sweep of just over 37 degrees, the 757 is swept at a relatively modest 25 degrees and the 767 just over 31 degrees. The 747 wing was designed for high-speed cruise over long ranges, whereas the 757 and 767 wings were both originally intended for short to medium range routes that do not need high cruise speeds. Even today, with the obvious exception of the supersonic Concorde, the 747-400 is still the fastest airliner with a cruise speed of Mach 0.85. Although the advanced wings of the 757 and 767 are highly efficient, they cruise at only Mach 0.8, which extends flight time on the long routes over which they—the 767 in particular—regularly fly. Airlines told Boeing they wanted the new jet to go faster.

Boeing therefore wanted to combine the efficiency of the new generation wings with the higher cruise capability of the 747. In the end, despite being swept back to within half a minute of the 767 at just over 31 degrees, the large 777 wing delighted Boeing by flying at Mach 0.84. Traditionally conservative Boeing estimated the wing would give the 777 a cruise speed of Mach 0.83 and the bonus speed was an unexpected extra from the flight tests.

Like the 757 and 767 wings, the 777 airfoil is supercritical. These are generally "fat" or relatively deep in cross-section and generate lift across their entire upper surface rather than in a concentrated area close behind the leading edge. In the case of the 777, the wing generates a lot of lift toward the

Although the 777 wing sweep angle is almost exactly the same as the 767 at just over 31 degrees, the new twinjet is capable of flying much faster at Mach 0.84 cruise speed. In shallow dives the test aircraft reached speeds of Mach 0.96.

"Flaperons" are mounted between the inboard and outboard flap sections and act as either ailerons or flaps, depending on the requirement. If folding wings were selected as an option on this aircraft, the wing-fold line would be located between the outboard end of the single-slotted trailing edge flap and the inboard end of the aileron at the wingtip.

trailing edge and is said to be "aft loaded." This is reflected in the scooped-out appearance of the underside of the wing near the trailing edge and is described as inverse, or aft, camber.

With the inherent aerodynamic efficiency of the new wing design, Boeing did not need winglets that are normally applied to an existing wing design to squeeze out more performance. However, in order to get the maximum out of the wing without using winglets, Boeing needed to keep the span as large as possible. Here it encountered a possible problem. The 777 was aimed at many of the airlines as a McDonnell Douglas DC-10 replacement. The gates at many of the airline's airport terminals were sized around the 165 foot (50.4m) wingspan of this popular trijet. How could Boeing combine the operating efficiency of a 200 foot (58.8m) span wing with the gate size of a 165 foot (50.3m) span aircraft? The answer was a folding wing like those used by carrier-based aircraft.

The hinge line for the wing fold is set at about 80 percent of the span, allowing the outer 22 feet (6.8m) to fold vertically upwards, reducing span to 155 feet (47.3m). The system can only be used when the aircraft is on the ground and traveling at less than 50 knots (58mph or 93km/h). Boeing designed the 777 wing-fold system along similar lines to that of the Northrop Grumman A-6 Intruder for which it developed a new composite-based wing. The 777 wingtip is connected with a hinge like a piano lid at the upper surface and a lug and clevis at the lower surface. Latch pins fasten the wing structurally in the spread position by pinning the outboard-hinge rib lugs to the inboard hinge rib lugs. Locks then fasten it in position.

By 1995, no operator had specified the folding-wing system, but Boeing is keeping it available as

The strake at the root of the horizontal tail is angled upward to align with the downwash of the local air flow and reduce drag.

sion loads experienced during flight. Aluminum is used for most of the wing internal structure, including the massive front and rear spars.

The flight control surfaces on the wing also differ from previous Boeing jetliners in some cases. The outboard leading edge slats, for example, are simpler than those of normal Boeing designs which normally use separate actuators to change the angle of the slat, as well as the support track that they run on. The 777 design has a one-piece circular arc slat track that drives and positions the slat in one movement. This is possible because designers contoured the outboard leading edge to fit the curved track and harks back to the original 1960s design of the 727 leading edge. The inboard and outboard trailing edge flaps are operated by a ball-screw drive, unlike the track and roller support or rotary actuator on other Boeing jetliners.

A crucial design element of the wing is the flaps. These play the biggest part in giving the 777 an exceptionally short takeoff and landing capability for such a large aircraft. A set of double-slotted flaps are positioned on the inboard trailing edge between the engine and the fuselage. The outer wing trailing edge supports a large, but simple, single-slotted flap section. The flaps can be moved to six positions. Extra help for takeoff and landing is provided by a high-speed aileron, which converts to a slotted flap for slow flight. A cove lip door seals the hinge gap when the "flaperon" (a combination of aileron and flap), is used as an aileron. This door opens to provide a smooth air flow when it is used as a flap, at which time it can be "drooped" down to 36 degrees. A set of seven spoilers and seven leading edge slats on each wing complete the slow flight ensemble.

Wheels and Tail

One of the few instantly recognizable external features of the 777 is its large main undercarriage. Adopted for the first time on any western-made jetliner, Boeing used the rather unusual six-wheel bogie design more commonly seen on the Tupolev Tu-154. The Menasco-built main gear has the advantage of spreading the aircraft's weight more evenly on the runway or taxiway surface, without the need for a

major fleets of DC-10s begin to change hands. The company also expects to offer the technology for the future New Large Airplane, which may need to fold its wings where gate size is restricted.

The huge wing also provides another vital ingredient to the 777 design goal, that of extra long range. All the 777-200 fuel is contained in the wing, with no tankage needed in the tail. The highest gross weight version of the 777-200, at 632,500 pounds (286,900kg) takes 44,700 gallons (169,200L) of fuel, giving a maximum range of up to 8,490 miles (13,669km). There is no fuel stored in the outboard section beyond the wing fold line.

The wing is skinned with a new Alcoa-developed aluminum alloy, 7055T77, which is best suited to the high compression, or squeezing loads, encountered on the upper surface of the wing. The lower wing surface is skinned with a 2000-series aluminum alloy which is resistant to the high ten-

third—or center—main gear leg. The 777 therefore has roughly the same "pavement loading" as the heavyweight intercontinental DC-10-30, but with 50 percent less parts and a lot less complexity. It also allows Boeing to grow the 777 into the stretch version without having to worry about adding extra legs, as McDonnell Douglas had to do when it developed the DC-10-30 out of the -10 series.

Unusually, the aft axle of the main gear can be steered up to 8 degrees in either direction to help with nose-gear steering. It also reduces the aircraft's turning radius and cuts down rubber loss, or "scrubbing" of the tires. Another benefit of the six-wheel arrangement is better wet-weather braking. This is simply due to improved traction and braking of the rear-most axle in the dried-out path of the first two main wheel sets. The brakes are controlled by digital autobrake and antiskid systems and individual brake temperatures can be monitored and displayed in the cockpit.

One of the less obvious but major design achievements of the 777 was the translating passenger door. The finely balanced door moves out and then sideways on a single hinge and can be moved with only one hand. The mechanism was the subject of a dedicated development and validation effort.

The main gear is the largest ever developed for any jetliner and eclipses even those of the 747 and Airbus A330/A340. To save some weight, the main truck is made from titanium but is otherwise conventional. A huge hydraulic actuator positions the main bogie to a 13 degree nose-up attitude for climb-out after takeoff and for landing. For retraction and stowage, the actuator moves the vast bulk of the gear to a 5 degree nose-down position.

The nose gear is very similar to that of the 767 but features some interesting additions to help the ground crew. Three lights tell the ground tug crew whether the aircraft's brakes are on or off, and a control panel on the back of the gear leg can also be used in an emergency to shut down the auxiliary power unit (APU) located in the tail.

Another distinguishing design feature is the "blade" tail cone. Recent findings in aerodynamics show that the traditional blunt-shaped tail generates induced drag. As a result, the tail cones of Boeing's jetliners have become gradually more and more pointed. Since the advent of both the 757 and 767, Boeing has discovered that a small amount of airflow becomes "stagnant" around conical tails so the 777 was formed into a sharper blade shape. Like most jetliners, the 777's APU is housed in the tail where there is the most volume of otherwise "useless" space and where the exhaust can be conveniently vented. Unlike most of the others which exhaust directly astern, however, Boeing has designed the 777 APU to exhaust through an outlet on one side of the blade tail.

The horizontal tail passes through the tail directly ahead of the APU. Unlike previous Boeing jetliners, in which the horizontal tail is usually made up of two tailplanes joined by a centerbox, the 777 tail is simply two tailplanes mated together in a giant "V." This occupies more space behind the pressure bulkhead but is easier, and therefore cheaper, to make. The incidence, or angle, of the entire tailplane can be adjusted using jacks to help keep the aircraft properly trimmed, or balanced. The tailplane can be moved up to 4 degrees upwards or 11 degrees downwards. The elevators on the trailing edge of the tailplane can move up to 30 degrees upwards and 25 degrees down.

CHAPTER 4

DIGITAL MASTERPIECE

The 777 is Boeing's first truly digital airliner. It uses an electronic "brain" to manage the most advanced avionics ever flown on a commercial airliner and is the first US-made jetliner to have fly-by-wire flight control. It has more than 2.6 million lines of software code incorporated in the avionics and cabin entertainment system, compared to 400,000 in the relatively sophisticated 747-400.

The "brain" is actually the aircraft information management system, or AIMS. The Honeywell-made AIMS is so advanced that versions of the system have been proposed for an upgrade to the USAF E-3 AWACS (airborne warning and control system),

The advanced cockpit is shown here to good effect as Boeing's Captain Ken Hiebert flies the 777-200 simulator. The flight deck is dominated by the main color flat-panel liquid-crystal displays (LCDs) which can be adjusted to show a huge variety of data ranging from the artificial horizon and weather radar to the health of the engines and the fuel system. Note the triple-channel autopilot with selectable flight path angle and track modes located above the main displays. The LCDs used in the simulator are early units and appear to be blotchy. Production standard units give a consistent display.

The two Aircraft Information Management System (AIMS) cabinets forming the heart of the 777's sophisticated avionics are located in the electronics bay beneath the flight deck. The entire nose section is "shielded" to protect sensitive electronics from electromagnetic interference such as lightning, microwave and radar transmitters, and even commercial radio transmitters.

and even for the Joint Strike fighter (JSF). The JSF program could provide the United States and other forces with a family of new tactical fighters early next century.

AIMS is new because it groups together most of the essential systems into one box. (In fact, there are two identical boxes, either of which can fly the 777 in case the other is somehow damaged.) Each contains flight management, flat panel cockpit display control, central maintenance, airplane condition monitoring, digital communication management, engine data interface, and a data conversion highway. All of these systems are normally self-contained LRUs (line replaceable units), but by being grouped together, can share the same power supply. In addition, they also use the same processors, memory system, operating system, utility software, hardware, built-in test equipment, and input/output ports.

By grouping everything together in this way, Boeing and Honeywell estimate that overall weight is cut by 20 percent and power requirement by around 30 percent. Most importantly, the reliability and ease of maintenance is drastically improved. Honeywell was able to group so many vital functions close together in safety because of advances in

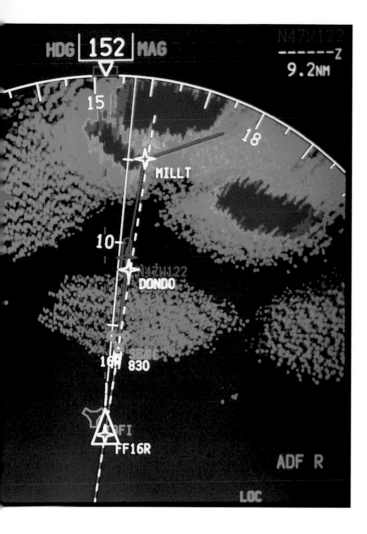

Active matrix LCDs are lighter, more reliable, and use less power. The primary flight display (left) shows the aircraft flying wings level at 133 knots (153mph or 246km/h) at an altitude of 1,480 feet on a heading of 152 degrees. The navigation display (right), shows a magenta line indicating the aircraft is inbound to the BFI (Boeing Field) beacon. Weather information is also overlaid.

speed and altitude. It builds on similar systems used in the 757, 767, and 747-400, but is more advanced with growth potential for expected use of satellite-based navigation and communication. All data is shown in the cockpit on color flat-panel displays. These liquid crystal displays (LCDs) are lighter and more reliable than the cathode ray tube, or TV-like displays, which ushered in the age of the "glass cockpit" to airliners in the 1980s and early 1990s.

The manufacturers faced a tough job to ensure the flat panel displays would be good enough for the job. They needed to be bright enough to be visible to the crew member on the other side of the cockpit, even with direct sunlight pouring in through the flightdeck windows. In addition, the quality of the actual image on the screen needed to be better than the high-resolution TV image of the standard instruments. Each of the six main LCD screens is eight-by-eight inches square (20cm x 20cm) and displays flight, navigation, and engine information. If one or more screens fail, then the others can take over and display any information the crew needs.

Another core system is called the central maintenance function (CMF). This checks virtually every system on board and flags up any maintenance requirements as they occur. The main reason for the CMF was to cut out the amount of trial and error, or "shotgun" maintenance, which often keeps an aircraft on the ground for hours while the real problems are located. A related system within AIMS is the airplane condition monitoring function which tracks and monitors engine and aircraft systems to provide a detailed database for airline use. The AIMS also contains a digital communications management function. This essentially provides a link between the aircraft and ground air traffic control networks as well as space-based satellite communications and navigation systems. This will become more and

"robust" partitioning between software. This means that different software, some of it flight critical, can be safely located in the same computer as nonflight critical code. The cabinets also built on advances in application specific integrated circuits (ASICs). These were vital to the system because they enabled the integration of more channel functions in a single processor channel. In other words, the system was doing more with less.

One of the main systems contained within AIMS is the flight management function. This is used to literally "manage" the flight and collects data from sensors to ensure that the 777 will cruise at the optimum

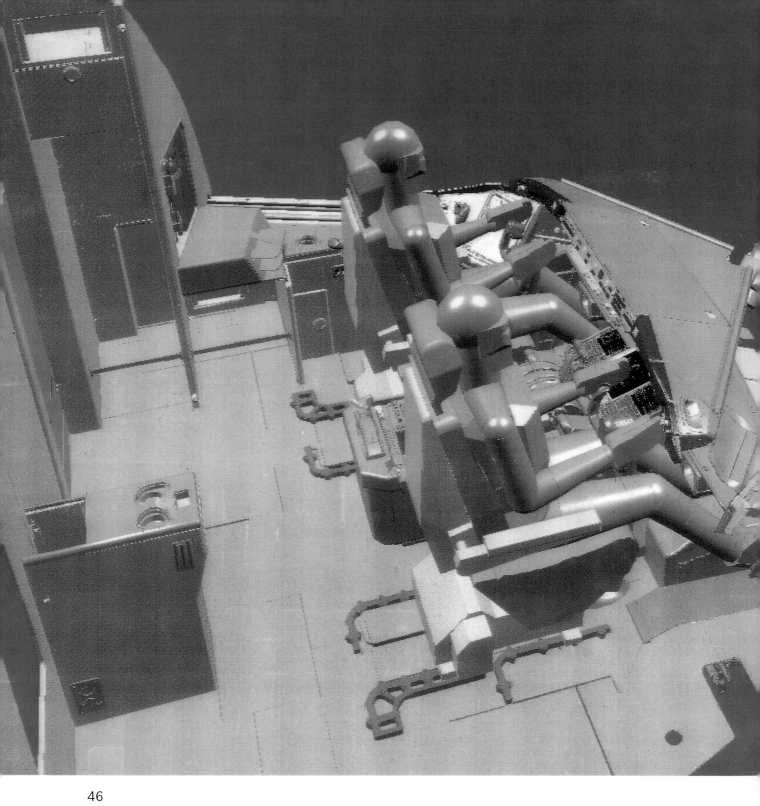

The fly-by-wire system protects the aircraft from banking too steeply, stalling, flying too fast, pitching too sharply, and helps the crew cope with the sudden loss of engine power on one side during critical times such as takeoff. Stalling speed at maximum takeoff weight for the early version of the -200 is around 177 knots (204mph or 328km/h). Stalling speed for the heavier B-market version is expected to be around 192 knots (221mph or 356km/h) under the same conditions.

more important to the 777 as the more advanced satellite navigation systems begin operation.

Just as a brain is connected to the rest of the body through the nervous system, so the AIMS is connected to the length and breadth of the 777 by a network of twisted wires called databuses. Known as the ARINC 629, each databus forms a bi-directional data highway that can ship up to two million bits per second. The ARINC 629 is like a telephone network because it allows two-way conversations between all the systems that are hooked up to it. A number of the older technology, one-way highways called the ARINC 429 are also used.

The 777 is also the first commercial aircraft to use fiber optic cables that may eventually replace the wire-based databus designs of today. The cables transmit high speed digital computer data to the

CATIA was used extensively to design the cockpit ergonomics. Here two CATIA "Robocops" try the seats out for size. *Boeing*

AIMS from a maintenance access terminal and side displays in the cockpit.

Also interfaced with AIMS is an autopilot/ flight director made by Collins Avionics. This is made up of three redundant computers, a control panel, and six backdrive control actuators. These provide a physical feedback to give the pilot some idea of the forces acting on the aircraft when a maneuver is made. Unlike a conventional aircraft, which is controlled with mechanical links between the flight control surfaces and the pilot's control column, the 777 uses a fly-by-wire, or electrically signaled flying control surfaces. There is therefore no direct physical feedback to the crew and artificial systems must be used instead. Collins also supplies LCD stand-by instruments and optional data management system side-display units.

The 777 is also crammed with very advanced sensing and navigational aids. One of these is a combined air data and inertial reference system, or ADIRS. At the heart of ADIRS are six tiny gyro-

The FBW system has a cross-tie between the wheel and the rudder that reduces sideslip during banked turns by adding small amounts of rudder. "Tail wag" during yaw is reduced by the automatic gust suppression system which applies rudder to oppose movement of the fin.

scopes made of glass. Laser beams shoot along hollowed-out cavities in the triangular-shaped glass and bounce off mirrors located at each corner of the triangle to complete their circuit, or ring. As the time taken for the light to travel around the triangle is fixed when the gyro is stationary, any slight changes in that time are the result of the gyro being moved. A computer can therefore calculate an aircraft's motion by comparing the time differences of several gyros. The 777's ring laser gyros (RLGs) are arranged in a skewed six-sided axis, instead of the normal right-angled pattern used in previous RLG systems.

The ADIRS also includes a secondary back-up source of motion sensing for the flight control system. This is based on fiber-optic gyros and is the first such application of such technology. Interferometric fiber-optic gyros (IFOGS) use light like ring laser gyros, but differ because the light travels through fiber-optic cable rather than through a vacuum. Light is sent in two directions along the fiber-optic pathway and, if any rotation takes place, the resulting difference in the beam can be measured.

Fly-By-Wire

Boeing had been keen to use fly-by-wire (FBW) on an airliner since studies carried out in the 1980s on an earlier project, the 7J7, had shown that big benefits were possible with a brand-new design. Boeing was also spurred on by high-tech competition from Airbus, which had flown the world's first fly-by-wire commercial transport—the A320—as far back as early 1987.

One of the immediate advantages of using FBW is weight saving; first, by replacing complicated linkages, cables, pulleys, brackets, and bellcranks with a wire which transmits electrical signals to the flying surfaces; and second, the computers at the core of a FBW system protect the airliner from heavy maneuvers and keep it stable at all times.

48

If the 777 is brought in for an automatic landing it will flare by itself at around 50 feet (15m) while the auto-throttle will begin to close at 25 feet (7.6m). The height of the flightdeck at touchdown is around 30 feet (9m).

This not only improves safety and efficiency, but also means that the basic airframe can be designed with lighter wing and tail structures.

Unlike a conventional aircraft, in which the flight control surfaces (like ailerons) are mechanically linked to the control column on the flightdeck, the 777 control surfaces are moved by the computers that interpret the pilot's commands. When the pilot pulls back on the control column, for example, the computers sense that he or she wants the aircraft to climb. The computer then activates the flight control surfaces to comply with these commands.

Three GEC-Marconi Avionics primary flight control computers form the core of the system. Each computer contains three different computing lanes. Each lane has a unique processor with its own power supply and access to the ARINC 629 databus. When the pilot moves the stick, the computer sends the relevant command to a unit called the actuator control electronics (ACE). Four ACEs work the actuators on the flying surfaces. Before the commands are sent, however, each channel in the computer checks its own command, as well as those

of its two counterparts. If all agree, the common command is sent to the ACEs. If one does not agree, it is overruled by the majority of channels.

Boeing and GEC performed rigorous testing of the FBW system and its software to ensure complete safety throughout the full flight envelope, and even beyond. The two companies concentrated not so much on the actual software but on the requirements that the code was written to meet. Experience of nearly every unexpected event with FBW aircraft in the past has shown that it is rarely the software that is the problem, but the original requirements themselves.

As far back as the late 1980s, the requirements for the control laws for the 777 were developed on a special aircraft that could be programmed to fly in a different way, depending on the flight control software. These were further refined in a simulator before being loaded into a specially modified 757. This was fitted with a switchable flight control system that could simulate the 777's FBW characteristics and was flown by several 777 test pilots, including John Cashman, who commanded the first flight. The requirements were further validated in the IASL and during 3,500 flight hours on the actual aircraft itself before the first 777 entered commercial service.

Software for the system was originally going to be written by three completely separate teams working independently to meet the same requirements. This is the same concept used by Airbus in the development of its FBW software. Boeing later changed its mind because the three teams were having to ask so many questions about the requirements that their independence was becoming compromised and similar logic was beginning to crop up in each solution. Boeing therefore switched to making

each computational lane within each computer slightly different as a way of maintaining integrity.

Though 777 pilots retain ultimate control, the flight control laws govern speed stability. This means that the aircraft is trimmed to a particular speed and any alteration from this speed causes a change in pitch to compensate. This differs from Airbus aircraft which are governed to maintain pitch, or pointing stability. If the 777 crew inadvertently let the speed drop close to a stall, for example, the computers send a nose-down command to the elevators and the nose will automatically drop to regain speed. If the crew

If the fly-by-wire system fails, the 777 can be safely flown back for a landing using the hydraulically controlled trim system on the horizontal stabilizer and one cable-driven spoiler on each wing. This system, which controls roll via spoilers, differs from the back-up mechanical system used by Airbus on its FBW airliners which controls yaw with rudder.

The leading edge of the tail is used to house various communications and navigation antennae. The high frequency (HF) transmit-and-receive antenna sits just below the VOR (VHF omni-directional radio) antenna, which is mounted in the front tip of the tail.

pulls back on the control column and then lets go, the column will go back to where it was.

The FBW system is also designed to protect the aircraft from "over-yawing." This could occur if one engine was not working or the crew was landing in a very strong crosswind. The system limits rudder deflection and allowed Boeing to keep down the size of the vertical tail. The system also stops the 777 from flying too fast in a dive, or from banking too steeply

(beyond 35 degrees). Another protection, which helps the pilot cope with the heavy workload of an engine failure on takeoff, is called the Thrust Asymmetry Compensation function. It automatically applies up to 10 degrees rudder when one engine gives more than 10 percent more power than the other.

The ACEs, developed by Lear Astronics and Teijin Seiki America, do not contain any software and are simply analog-to-digital devices that transfer a pilot's control input into an order to the actuator to move the flight control surface. In the event of a total primary computer failure, the ACEs can be used to control the aircraft. If everything in the FBW system fails, the crew has an old-fashioned mechanically linked backup control to get them home. This consists of the hydraulically controlled trim system on the horizontal stabilizer in the tail, made by E-Systems, and one cable-driven spoiler on each wing surface.

Flightdeck and Other Systems

The 777 "front office" is an advanced mixture of the 747-400 and the 767. Most of the avionics architecture is based on the bigger Boeing, but the systems are more similar to its fellow twinjet, the 767. Like many other "market driven" aspects of the 777, the flightdeck was designed with input from almost 600 aircrew from airlines, vendors, industry, and regulatory authorities.

More than 1,500 flight hours were "logged" by 33 Boeing pilots in special simulators built within the IASL complex. Perhaps surprisingly, few wanted the side-stick controllers which are featured on aircraft as diverse as the Lockheed Martin F-16 and Airbus A340. Boeing preferred the extra feedback and situational awareness the full-size control column gives to the pilot.

The 777 flightdeck accommodates all sorts and sizes of pilots ranging in height from 5'2" to 6'4", and has adjustable rudder pedals. Other new features to help the crew include an electronic checklist that is accessed with a cursor control. Another "first" on the commercial flightdeck is an interactive touch-activated screen.

Of the major systems controlled from the cockpit one of the most vital is the electrics. The 777 consumes a vast amount of power because of all the new cabin entertainment systems, the FBW flight controls, and larger ovens. In previous Boeings, the electronic bays dissipate up to 14kVA; whereas, the in-flight entertainment system alone in the 777 consumes up to 22kVA. Power comes from three big generators, two of which are strapped to the engines. A third is attached to the auxiliary power unit (APU) in the tail.

A sophisticated electrical loads monitoring system, which sheds loads one by one in case of power loss, is made by Smiths Industries to control the electrical system. More power is also taken from the engines off another shaft using a variable-speed constant frequency system made by Sundstrand. Three permanent magnets attached to the same shaft provide power for the FBW system. If all power fails, the crew can drop the ram-air turbine. This can be dropped out into the airstream from the wingroot fairing of the 777 in case of emergency.

Other systems, like those for the hydraulics and fuel, show strong resemblance to the 767. Each of the three independent, 3,000 pound-per-square-inch (207bar) hydraulic systems is powered with pumps driven from the engines and generators and bleed air in combinations designed to minimize the effect of power source failures on the hydraulic system. As an indication of how big the 777 and its demands have become since the beginning of the program, the AlliedSignal-built air drive unit, which drives the central hydraulic system, is 45 percent more powerful than the unit first proposed by Boeing. An unusual feature of the fuel system is the fuel quantity indicating system developed by Smiths Industries. This uses ultrasonic sensors in the tanks to measure volume and mass and presents the information via the ARINC 629 on flightdeck displays.

A new type of air-conditioning system, which is the first to use a lighter condensing-cycle technology, has been developed by Hamilton Standard. The same company also produces ice-protection for the wings and engines. Hamilton Standard and AlliedSignal jointly produce an ozone converter that removes contaminants from the cabin air. The rest of the environmental control and the ram-air turbine is supplied by AlliedSignal.

The AIMS and FBW system depend on air data sensors to enable them to operate. A cluster of sensors, including the stall warning device located on the green stripe, are mounted around the nose of the aircraft. The antenna for another vital piece of the avionics suite, the Traffic Alert and Collision Avoidance System (TCAS), is just visible on the roof of the aircraft above the cabin door.

CHAPTER 5

THE WORLD'S BIGGEST ENGINES

The engine makers faced a huge challenge to develop powerplants for the 777. The engines not only needed to be the biggest ever made, but each would have to be developed, tested, and delivered in record time.

To make matters worse, the 777 was launched during the lead into the most severe recession ever experienced by the aerospace industry. Engine makers would have to compete aggressively for a share of a stagnant market to get any hope of getting back some of the millions of dollars poured into power-

Right
The GE90 fan blades are made from composite material, unlike those of the competitors, which are composed of titanium. Each blade is, however, fitted with a titanium leading edge to improve resistance to impact from stones, grit, or birds that may be sucked in on takeoff or landing. Note the aluminum spacers between each blade root, which were redesigned later in the program.

Left
British Airways engineers at London Heathrow get to grips with the huge size of the GE90 during the first visit of the General Electric-powered 777 to the UK in late April 1995.

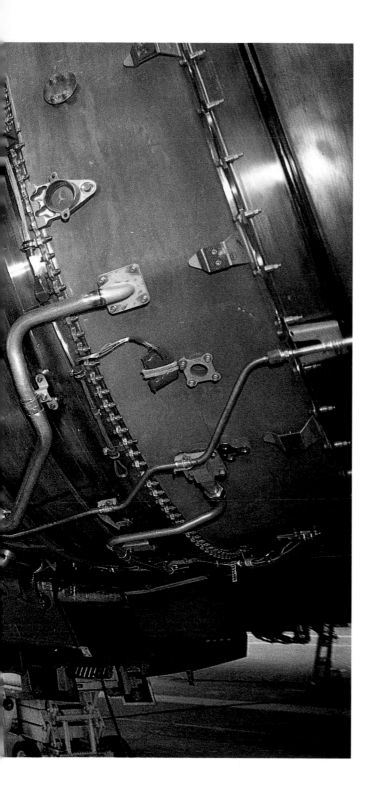

Hidden beneath the smooth external nacelle of the GE90 lies the complex-looking core and accessories. Here, engineer Will Greenfield works on the left engine of the first GE90-powered 777 at Boeing Field during the certification program.

plant development. Added to this was the demanding task of producing the engines "service ready" and ETOPS qualified.

The engines are easily the most impressive external feature of the 777. Each can suck in around two million cubic feet of air per minute at takeoff power. Even though they already are the most powerful commercial aircraft engines ever built, they will continue to grow in thrust capability by as much as a third again as the aircraft is stretched and gains weight throughout its career.

On early model 777-200s, each engine generates more than 75,000 pounds (333kN) of thrust compared to about 56,000 pounds (250kN) for a current 747 engine. Added together, the combined takeoff thrust of the 777's engines is therefore around 150,000 pounds (667kN). This will eventually rise to more than 200,000 pounds (890kN) as the heavier and stretched versions are developed.

GE90

Of the three big engine makers competing on the 777, General Electric (GE) took the biggest gamble by announcing in January 1990 that it was designing an all-new engine for the twin. GE believed that the new technology of the engine, dubbed the GE90, would give it performance benefits over the competing powerplants, including fuel savings estimated at around $300,000 per year, per aircraft.

To the surprise of the world's aerospace industry, GE signed up British Airways, a formerly loyal Rolls-Royce user, as launch customer. British Airways, which ordered 15 firm 777s and took 15 options, was widely tipped to order the Trent for its new twinjet.

The GE90 is the largest of the three engines offered on the 777. Its 10.25 foot (3.1m) diameter fan, plus the extra few inches for the external cowling, is wider than the fuselage of the first generation Boe-

Two views of the sturdy engine mount. Note the large gap between the inner and outer rings which indicates the exceptionally high bypass ratio of the GE90.

ing jetliners. GE designed the fan this large to produce a high bypass ratio. Bypass ratio is the amount of air traveling through the fan duct divided by the airflow through the central core where the jet reaction takes place. As a result, the GE90's bypass ratio is more than 9 to 1 compared to the 5 to 1 typically found in most current "big fan" jet engines.

The huge fan helps produce an overall pressure ratio of more than 40 to 1. The pressure ratio measures the difference in pressure between the outside air and the gas exiting the compressor of the engine. The large size of the fan meant that each blade had to be made out of lightweight composite materials. These were the first large-scale fan blades to be made out of composites and were fitted with a titanium cuff to protect the leading edge of each blade from impact damage from objects sucked into the engine during

A peek up the "business end" of the powerful P&W engine. The evening sunlight picks out the split in the casing at the bottom center where it can be divided to provide maintenance access. High temperature-resistant inconel is used to cover parts of the underside of the strut connecting the engine to the wing.

takeoff, such as grit, stones, and even birds. For the first time on a GE turbofan, the blades were of a wide chord design to improve their pumping efficiency.

Snecma, GE's French partner on the successful CFM56 engine, produces the GE90's high-pressure compressor for the two-shaft engine. This is a 10-stage design derived from a joint NASA/GE project called the Energy Efficient Engine (E3) which took place in the 1980s. The GE90 also has a new type of combustor known as a dual-dome. This is arranged in a ring, or annulus, around the engine core and consists of two major zones of combustion. When the engine is at low power, or idle thrust, only one "dome" is lit. The use of one dome cuts down the amount of time any unburned fuel spends in the combustor and therefore reduces the emissions of carbon monoxide and hydrocarbons by up to 50 percent. At higher power levels, the second dome kicks in. The unit is designed to cut emissions of nitrogen oxides by 35 percent and smoke emissions by 50 percent.

GE ran the first core engine on November 24, 1992. Four months later the company ran the first full fan-equipped engine and on April 3, 1993, reached a record thrust level of 105,400 pounds (468kN). By the end of 1993, the engine was flying on GE's specially adapted, ex-Pan Am 747-100 testbed from Mojave, California.

Like its competitors, the GE90 suffered its share of teething troubles, most of which were un-

The inlet guide vanes are clearly visible behind the wide chord hollow titanium fan blades of this PW4077. The 777 engine was Pratt & Whitney's first commercial application of wide-chord fan technology.

Sunlight illuminates the rotating fan and yellow painted spinner on this Rolls-Royce Trent as a Cathay Pacific 777 comes in to land at Boeing Field on a late summer evening in 1995. The spiraling effect of the painted spinner is believed to alarm birds, causing them to fly away from the aircraft.

April showers gather close by as a Pratt & Whitney PW4084-powered 777 in United livery visits Heathrow for the first time in 1995. Although physically identical, the 77,000-pound thrust version of the engine is also known as the PW4077, while the derated 74,000 pound thrust version is known as the PW4074. Engine power can be increased or decreased by changing the settings in the electronic engine control.

The curved titanium fan blades of the Rolls-Royce Trent rotate clockwise like most propellers, unlike the P&W and GE engines which turn counter-clockwise. Note the collar mounted behind the spinner, which was added to improve airflow into the core of this big engine. Rolls-Royce was the first engine maker to develop wide-chord fan-blade technology. It is also the only western engine maker to use a three-shaft design.

clearances in the compressor and revised the design. Despite these incidents, GE remained confident that the GE90 would perform to specification and, as if to underline this, accelerated plans to certify the growth engine at 92,000 pounds (410kN).

Finally, after the long awaited Federal Aviation Administration (FAA) ticket was granted, the first GE90-powered 777-200 took to the air on February 2, 1995, more than two months later than planned due to complications over the certification of the engine. These were mainly caused by the large amount of testing that went into clearing the GE90's composite fan for flight testing on the 777. The bodies of dead birds weighing, in one case, up to 8 pounds (3.6kg) were fired at the revolving fan to simulate the effect of a bird-strike on takeoff. Another severe test involved the deliberate release of a blade when the fan was rotating at 2,485 rpm and the engine producing more than 105,000 pounds (467kN) of thrust. An explosive charge at the base of the blade was detonated to simulate the effect of a breaking blade. Although severely damaged, the engine case contained the flying debris and the effect on other blades was within limits.

The fan blades were to remain a contentious issue for GE right through the early flight test and certification of the 777. Test flying of the GE90-powered aircraft for British Airways was temporarily halted at one point as engineers worked to redesign small spacers between the roots of the blades. In birdstrike tests on the 92,000 pound (409kN) version, the roots of adjacent blades were damaged when the spacer—or platform—moved sideways as the target blade was hit. GE fixed the problem by making the spacer more frangible so that it would not bite into the roots of the other blades.

After overcoming futher certification issues related to icing British Airways received the first

covered by the 747 testbed. At one stage the high-pressure turbine (HPT) blades rubbed against the casing, which resulted in part of the engine being shipped back to Ohio. Clearances between the HPT blades and casing were increased slightly as a result. Another problem occurred later in the same area when high acoustic vibration levels caused cracking in the HPT mid-seal. This was fixed with a "damper" to tone out the vibration. The design of the combustor was also slightly altered when the unit's center body suffered "distress."

Toward the end of the first scheduled set of 747 testbed flights, a fourth stage low-pressure compressor blade failed. This was traced to an earlier "rub" when the blade had been stressed after coming into contact with the compressor wall. GE increased

The strut box structure exposed on this engineless All Nippon Airways aircraft is attached to the wing by a system of links, braces, and struts designed to withstand limit loads if any single part fails. However, in a return to the original design philosophy of the 707, these are also designed so that in the event of an extreme overload, the strut will separate from the wing without damaging the wing box itself.

GE90-powered 777s in November 1995. British Airways is also set to take delivery of the first growth-version of the GE90 for use on its higher gross weight B-market 777-200s in December 1996. Although the engine is to be certified at 92,000 pounds (409kN), British Airways will probably operate the engine "de-rated" at around 90,000 pounds (400kN). GE ultimately plans to develop a family of engines from the GE90 ranging in thrust right up to around 115,000 pounds (511kN).

Within weeks of delivery of the first GE90-powered 777, GE received a huge boost when it was formally selected by the Saudi Arabian Airline Corporation (Saudia) to power 23 777-200s. Like most of the later BA aircraft, the Saudia fleet will be powered by the 92,000 pound (410KN) thrust GE90-92B version.

PW4084

Pratt & Whitney's PW4084 turbofan was chosen by United Airlines, the launch customer for the

Thrust reversers are activated on this GE90-powered 777 as it runs up to full thrust during a preflight test at Boeing Field.

777, and was therefore the first engine to power the aircraft for its maiden flight on June 12, 1994. Pratt & Whitney (P&W) decided to stick to a more powerful version of the successful PW4000 family, rather than go for an all-new powerplant. The strategy was low risk, offered high reliability, and was aimed at meeting the Boeing and United goal of entering operation as "service ready" as possible.

Rated at 77,200 pounds (343kN) thrust for United, and certified at 84,600 pounds (376kN) takeoff thrust, the PW4084 became the most powerful engine to ever be used in commercial aviation when it entered service on the London to Washington, D.C., route in June 1995. Most of the extra power comes from the 9.3 foot (2.8m) diameter fan, some 18 inches (45cm) bigger than the fan used by its PW4000-series relatives that power the 747 and MD-11. Like GE, P&W opted to use a wide chord fan for the new engine and developed blades made from hollow titanium.

P&W began work on the PW4084 in 1989 and by July 1992 had assembled the first engine that ran at a thrust level of more than 90,000 pounds (400kN) a month later. In November 1993, the PW4084 was flown on the prototype 747, which Boeing leased from a Seattle-based museum to act as a testbed. On its third test flight it suffered three surges just after takeoff. A surge is the nearest equivalent to a belch,

or backfire. It occurs when the flow of air through part of the engine is suddenly reversed.

In this case, the problem was found to be a tiny gap that opened up between the compressor and the surrounding casing. This was caused by the case expanding (due to heat) faster than the compressor rotor and was cured by limiting the amount of cooling air being fed to the rotor. In February 1994, another problem cropped up when the engine damaged one of the supports on the test stand as it quickly decelerated after a fan blade-off test. P&W stiffened the engine casing to make sure that any torque, or twisting, would be safely contained by the engine and not transmitted to the engine attachments.

The test was the toughest ever performed according to the three commercial engine makers that submitted engines. In P&W's case, 22 engines were dedicated entirely to the testing process. For certification, the engines were run for a total of more than 2,500 hours and the equivalent of 6,000 takeoffs and landings. Flocks of dead birds and single birds weighing up to 8 pounds (3.6kg) were fired into the rotating engine at more than 200mph (320km/h). All the engines had to endure the blade-off test that results in the detached blade smashing into the containment ring around the engine with a force equal to a car hitting a wall at 80mph (128km/h). Water simulating rainfall of

28 inches per hour (71cm/h), or a one-in-a-billion storm, was funneled through the engine. For some tests the engine was deliberately made to run out of balance and run at twice the vibration level allowed.

In spite of the early problems, the engine performed well and proved to be highly reliable. In fact, by the time the 777 flight test program began, there was so much confidence in the PW4084 that the crew shut one engine down and then relit it on the first flight. Meanwhile, P&W began development of a more powerful version, the 90,000 pound (400kN) PW4090 for heavier B-market 777-200s and completed manufacture of the first of the new version on July 14, 1995.

An even larger version, the 98,000 pound (436kN) thrust PW4098 was also announced in 1995. This is destined for the heaviest 777-200s and the stretched 777-300 which weighs slightly more with a gross takeoff weight of around 660,000 pounds (299,370kg) . The engine was selected by Korean Air Lines, All Nippon, and Japan Airlines when the stretch was publicly announced at the 1995 Paris Air Show. The PW4098 is expected to be certified for the 777-300 around September 1997, some 14 months after the PW4090.

Trent 800

Like P&W, Rolls-Royce preferred the less risky approach of developing a 777 engine from an existing family. In this case Rolls developed the Trent 800 and the Trent 768 (for the Airbus A330) from the RB211-524G and H used on the 747-400 and 767.

Following the RB211 family tradition, the Trent is a three-shaft engine, unlike the GE90 and PW4084, which are both two-shaft designs. Like the other engines, the Trent has a fan, a high-pressure compressor, and a high- and low-pressure turbine. However, the extra shaft connects an intermediate eight-stage compressor with an intermediate turbine. Rolls maintains the extra "intermediate" shaft means that the various speeds of all three shafts are much more closely matched to the actual work they are performing. Rolls also believes that for this reason, the more powerful the engine, the more applicable the three-shaft principle.

Because the three-shaft engine is usually more compact, and stubbier, than the longer two-shaft en-

The APU exhaust system is designed to minimize the possibility of "back pressure" to the APU, which would cause it to surge. It also prevents hot gas from searing the side of the aircraft and leaving large soot stains. The side-mounted exhaust also cuts down the amount of noise from the APU and prevents it from ingesting snow, ice, and anti-ice fluids.

gines, it does not "bow" or "flex" so much when thrust settings change. Rolls believes this factor helps maintain good engine performance longer and slows degradation down. In the past, one of the major drawbacks about the compactness of the family has been its associated weight. The RB211 family has traditionally been substantially heavier than its competitors. The Trent 890, however, is actually the smallest of the three 777 engines and is also the lightest.

Rolls was the first engine maker to ever use wide chord fans and has refined this technology for the

Trent. The 9.3 foot (2.8m) diameter fan is made up of 26 blades made from hollow titanium. These are made using a technique called superplastic forming and diffusion bonding which involves layering sheets of titanium together. The sheets are then welded closed around three edges to form an envelope. Inert gas is then pumped into the open end of the "envelope" to inflate it and form the hollow blade.

The Trent engine series was launched for the A330 and 777 in 1988, with the first run in August 1990. Thai Airways became the launch customer for the Trent 800, followed by Cathay Pacific, Emirates, and Singapore Airlines which placed a huge order for up to 61 Rolls-powered 777s in November 1995. Rolls completed design of the 800 in 1993 with the first engine run later that year. In early 1994 it became obvious to Rolls that the weight of the 777 was growing as airlines wanted more payload and range. As a result, Rolls decided to raise certification thrust from 84,000 pounds (373kN) to 90,000 pounds (400kN) and to accelerate the development program by three months. The company achieved these goals and became the first manufacturer to be cleared for flight at 90,000 pounds (400kN) in January 1995.

Rolls Royce had hoped to avoid the need to fly on Boeing's 747 engine testbed, but the unexpected experiences of the GE90 and PW4084 flight tests convinced Boeing, and particularly its test pilots, that it was necessary. The Trent 890 duly made 20 hours flying time mounted on the 747 during the spring of 1995.

The first Trent 890-powered 777 made its maiden flight from Paine Field, at Everett on May 27, 1995, in the colors of Cathay Pacific. The flight lasted 5.5 hours during which the 777 reached 33,000 feet and a cruising speed of Mach 0.6 (or around 420mph). The initial flight included violent "slam" engine accelerations and decelerations and engine relights, all of which were successfully completed.

However, when the aircraft landed at Boeing Field after the first flight, engineers were surprised to find small cracks in an aerodynamic fairing over the aft end of the strut which holds the engine to the wing. Boeing is responsible for the entire propulsion package including the nacelles and strut and worked to redesign a stronger covering. The process

held up test flying for around one month and the program finally resumed in early July.

Rolls meanwhile is busy working on a 95,000 pound (422kN) growth version, the Trent 895, which will power the first Cathay Pacific 777-300 in May 1998. Thai was meanwhile set to become the first Trent-777 operator when it took delivery in early 1996.

AlliedSignal 331-500 APU

The most unglamorous engine in any aircraft is the auxiliary power unit. However, the APU is a vital part of the 777 even though it is not used for propulsion. The APU pumps power into aircraft systems and is essential for helping restart engines, particularly in an emergency. Unfortunately the APU itself is often hard to start in many aircraft. It sits in the tail where it freezes in "cold soak" at high cruise altitude for hours until it is needed just before landing.

Because the APU was so important to the "service ready" initiative and to obtaining early ETOPS, AlliedSignal has designed new features into it to make sure that it will start 99 percent of the time by the second attempt. These include two starter motors, one electric and the other pneumatic. It also has electric bearing and gearbox heaters to stir cold sludgy oil and a much more powerful 40-amp battery. The APU also uses a two-stage compressor that is easier to start than the standard single-stage unit. AlliedSignal invested around $70 million in the 331-500, compared to $30 million for previous APUs.

The extra investment also covered an unparalleled test program, which saw more than 10,000 hours on the APU by the time it entered service, compared to around 2,500 hours for the 757 and 767.

The tight schedule of the 777 flight test program gave a lot of business to outsize cargo aircraft like this Heavylift-Volga Dnepr Antonov An-124. Such were the time limits involved, that engines often needed to be shipped complete with nacelle to save time, and the An-124 was perfect for this role. In service, 777 operators will be able to break engines down into modules for shipment on smaller aircraft. The photo shows the arrival of a GE90 engine at Boeing Field after modification at Cincinnati, Ohio, in June 1995.

CHAPTER 6

FLIGHT TEST

The first 777 off the Everett production line was rolled out amid enormous celebrations on April 9, 1994. The aircraft was unveiled, rather than rolled out, at half' hourly intervals to allow up to 100,000 Boeing workers, families, friends, and guests to share in the celebrations.

Amid the razzmatazz, Boeing engineers were working flat out with their suppliers to ready the big bird for its first flight, which was set for the beginning of June. Last-minute checks to the critical flight-control software and AIMS added to concerns that the tight schedule might slip. These were compounded by late changes to the engine. To get the completed flight-worthy engines to Boeing in time, P&W was even forced to charter a giant Russian-made Antonov An-124 to fly the podded powerplants from its East Hartford factory in Connecticut to Everett in Washington.

After what appeared to be super-human efforts by all concerned, the 777, WA001, moved under its

Hollywood comes to Everett as the 777 is unveiled with a fanfare of special effects on April 9, 1994. *Boeing*

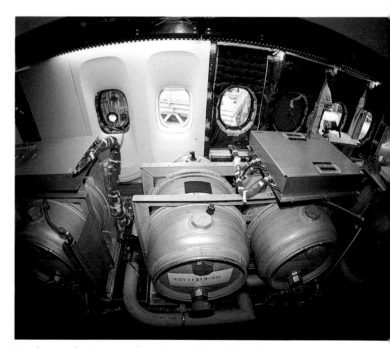

To change the center of gravity and simulate the weight of passengers and baggage, water was pumped around 48 keg-shaped barrels in the cabin of the test aircraft.

More than 20 banks of consoles and instruments collected around 50,000 measurements of avionics, electrical signals, hydraulic pressures, temperatures, air speed, and altitude. The data system weighed around 34,000 pounds (15,450kg) and included more than 100 miles (160km) of wire.

own power for the first time in May and began taxi tests. Within days, everything was ready apart from the weather. Finally, on June 12, a slight improvement set the stage for the long awaited first flight of the most comprehensive testing effort in commercial aviation history. In all, nine 777s would eventually be used in the certification flight effort which would run from June 1994 to early 1996. This would cover more than 4,900 flights totaling 7,000 hours, compared with 1,380 hours for the 757 and 1,790 hours for the 767.

To abide by international safety rules, the first takeoff had to be made away from built-up areas, which in the case of Everett's Paine Field, is to the north. Providing an additional challenge, a fresh southerly tailwind was gusting down the runway at up to 15 knots (17mph or 28km/h) as 777 Chief Pilot John Cashman and Director of Flight Test Ken Higgins lined up. Due to the tailwind, the throttles were pushed forward to 77,000 pounds (342kN) thrust for each engine, instead of the 74,000 pounds (329kN) originally planned. The big twin accelerated effortlessly and lifted off toward the overcast flanked by the Boeing chase plane.

The 3-hour-48 minute maiden flight, a record for an all-new Boeing jetliner, was judged a great success. Cashman reported that the prototype 777 handled better than many new production aircraft he had taken for first-check flights. Only two failures were reported on the aircraft itself, while another occurred with the fin-mounted trailing sensor cone which could not be retracted for landing. The only unexpected event was some vibration from the nose undercarriage doors during one of the cycling tests of the gear at high speeds. This was soon rectified on later flights. Unusual for a first flight, the left engine was shut down at 15,000 feet and 240 knots (276mph or 445km/hr). It was allowed to cool and then restarted with a windmilling re-light. From the start, a quiet confidence exuded from the test team. One hint was the test card for

Left
Under a sullen Washington sky, the 777 took off for its maiden flight at 11:45 a.m. on June 12, 1994. The aircraft reached 19,000 feet during the 3-hour 48-minute flight. *Boeing*

Right
Boeing's original 747 prototype, "City of Everett," was brought out of retirement to act as an engine testbed for the 777. It tested the Pratt & Whitney and Rolls-Royce engines whilst GE used its own ex-Pan Am 747 as a flying testbed for the GE90.

the nail-biting first flight. Amongst the 43 test conditions that were achieved on the flight, #42 was perhaps the most unusual. It stated: "Taxi back. Try real hard not to smile too much."

The early flight-test aircraft contained 22 racks of computer consoles and instruments capable of collecting more than 50,000 different measurements of aircraft data. The data systems weighed up to 34,000 pounds (15,300kg) and included more than 100 miles (161km) of wiring. The aircraft were also fitted with 48 barrels, divided evenly between the front and aft ends. These simulated various center-of-gravity changes as well as the weight of passengers and baggage. They contained water, though many were decorated with labels from Seattle's famous micro-breweries.

Test flying continued at a furious pace and by August the first aircraft was at Edwards AFB, California, for ground effect tests. In October, WA001 returned to the Mojave Desert where it underwent minimum unstick speed tests on Edwards' long runways. Designed to determine the lowest speed for a given weight at which the aircraft can takeoff, the pilots deliberately "tailscraped" the 777, which was fitted with a laminated-oak skid to protect the tail.

The aircraft later completed refused takeoff tests at Edwards and Roswell Airport, New Mexico. The ultimate test involved WA001 accelerating down the Edwards main 15,000 foot (4,575m) runway at more than 200mph with engines set at 88,000 pounds (391kN) thrust. The engines were suddenly throttled back and the aircraft, ballasted to its maximum takeoff weight of 632,500 pounds (287,150kg), was braked to an emergency stop. The brakes, which were purposely worn to the point of replacement,

By October 1994, WA001 was racing through the test card. It completed the first major FAA certification test when it performed all nine Vmu (velocity minimum unstick) speeds, which determine the aircraft's minimum takeoff speed. Note the smoke coming from the wooden tail skid. *Boeing*

A United test aircraft surges through a specially laid water trough to examine the spray pattern of a water splash. *Boeing*

stopped the aircraft in 1,400 feet (427m) less than was expected. The aircraft then sat with brakes glowing an orangy-red for five minutes to simulate the time taken for airport fire crews to reach it.

The flight tests were not without unexpected incidents and results. At one stage a temporary ceiling limit of 25,000 feet was placed on it by the FAA after two incidents of cabin decompression occurred within hours of each other in February 1995. The two incidents, one in Hawaii and the other in Seattle, were related to the failure of a check valve in the air conditioning system. A modified duct clamp was developed as a result, and the ceiling lifted. Flight testing also revealed a steeper than expected roll-off to the left during the approach to a stall with flaps down. This was corrected with a small change in the flight control software.

Most of the test flying was based out of Boeing Field and former Strategic Air Command bases such as the one in Glasgow, Montana. However, occasionally the test fleet would scour the world in search of freezing or boiling temperatures to adequately test all the on-board systems. The aircraft froze in Alaska and Sweden and baked in Arizona and New Mexico.

It was not all " smooth sailing" for the test effort. Here a 777 awaits modified GE90 engines after changes were found to be needed to the aluminum fan platform and to the engine control software.

One 777 even sweated in Florida where it was sent for "rain in the plane" humidity testing. It later returned to Seattle when it was realized that the inside test could be performed just as well using 40 humidifiers located throughout the cabin.

It's a busy scene on the Boeing Field test ramp as N7772 is prepared for another sortie. Note the extended cable of the air data sensor, the open APU access doors beneath the tail, and the highlighted translating doors.

Flight testing proceeded so quickly that an aircraft was released for a world tour in April 1995. The 777 flew 45,890 miles (73,883km) on the 10-nation tour taking in Korea, China, Hong Kong, Taiwan, UK, South Africa, India, Malaysia, Singapore, and Thailand. On its return to Seattle, the aircraft established a world-speed record on the 7,850-mile (12,638km) nonstop flight from Bangkok. Another world-speed record was achieved on June 11, 1995, when a 777, the first ETOPS-dedicated aircraft, flew 5,142 miles (8,278km) from Seattle to the Paris Air Show in 9 hours, 2 minutes.

Three United 777s that were involved in the test program were refurbished before being formally delivered back to the airline. United experienced a rapid build-up in deliveries with 11 in 1995 and a scheduled rate of around one per month until 1999.

ETOPS

One of the major planks of the 777 program was Boeing's radical "Early ETOPS" initiative which would certify it to fly up to 180 minutes from a suitable alternative airport at entry into service. On December 29, 1994, the fourth 777 began a special 1,000-flight effort which was dedicated to achieving the Early ETOPS goal.

Backed by thousands of test hours at the IASL, and at the engine and systems suppliers facilities, the 1,000 flights were the equivalent of more than a year of flights for a typical airline. More than 1,400 hours were built up during the flights, which varied from one hour to

WA102, the Rolls-Royce Trent 800 ETOPS 1,000-cycle validation aircraft, was well into the rigorous program by late 1995.

more than nine. Also included were eight 180-minute single-engine diversions for a total of 24 hours, which equals the same number of diversion hours accumulated by the first five years of 767 ETOPS service.

For the last 90 of the 1,000 flights, the airline became directly involved by simulating normal airline operations with a test aircraft. On April 1, 1995, United flight and ground crews joined Boeing personnel on a flight from Los Angeles to Washington to mark the beginning of the 90 flights. In the case of the United-P&W ETOPS qualification, this included flights to Honolulu, Los Angeles, Denver, Miami, and Washington, D.C. The GE-powered 777 effort was led by British Airways, which flew flights on routes linking London with cities in the Middle East as well as Washington, D.C., and Newark, New Jersey. The Rolls-Royce Trent ETOPS

81

Excluding ETOPS testing, the P&W-powered 777 test fleet built up 2,092 dedicated flight-test hours before certification on April 19, 1995, compared to 1,793 for the 767 program.

The British Airways GE90-777 ETOPS aircraft was due to complete its 1,000 cycle validation tests in early 1996. By August 1995, the engine had built up 300 flight hours on the 777 and 228 on GE's 747 flying testbed. Some 15,000 engine cycles (simulating a full flight from start-up to turn off) had also been accumulated during ground and flight tests. Most of the early test hours were logged on this aircraft, G-ZZZA.

plan involved Cathay Pacific, which flew it from Hong Kong to Sydney and Singapore.

Ultimately, the P&W-powered 777 became the first Boeing jetliner to obtain simultaneous certification from both the FAA and the European Joint Aviation Authorities (JAA) when it was approved on April 19, 1995. Just under a month later, on May 15, the first 777 was handed over to United at a ceremony on the ramp outside Seattle's Museum of Flight. Appropriately named "Working Together," the first United 777 was saluted by the identically named WA001, which performed a spectacular low-level fly-by.

With just days to go before the 777 entered service, the FAA granted it 180 minutes ETOPS. The European JAA, which has jurisdiction over aircraft registered with member nations, granted 120 minutes at entry-into-service. Finally, on June 7, 1995, a United 777-200 left London Heathrow bound for Washington, D.C., on the type's first-ever scheduled service. Loaded with VIPs and, to United's relief, some fare-paying passengers, Flight No. 921 landed at Dulles Airport some 30 minutes ahead of schedule. Five years after the "Working Together" pledge was signed, the age of the 777 had finally begun.

THE
FUTURE
FAMILY

The 777 is quickly becoming one of the most versatile jetliners ever developed. Its flexible design, combined with the huge power capability of the new engines specially developed for the new twin, gives Boeing the chance to beef-up, shrink, and stretch the 777.

According to the original plan, the initial A-market versions replace older trijets on transcontinental

Right
Two of the original "gang of eight," British Airways and Cathay Pacific, will remain loyal users of the 777 throughout its career. Cathay was a leading advocate of the stretch and was among the early group of Asian-based carriers that helped launch the program in June 1995. The Hong Kong airline converted seven of 11 existing 777-200 orders to the new version, the first of which it will take in around May 1998. British Airways, with up to thirty 777s on order and option, is expected to be interested in the -300 as a long-term replacement for its fleet of 747-100/200 "Classics."

Left
A sight guaranteed to become increasingly common in the late 1990s, a 777 takes on cargo before another long-range flight. By late-1995, Boeing claimed that since its launch in October 1990, the 777-200 had captured more than 70 percent of the market for aircraft in its size category.

Although the 737-400 is a relatively new member of the little twinjet family, almost 27 years separates the first flights of the 737-100 and the 777-200. By 1995, the growing order book for the 777 and the Next Generation 737 family promised at least two decades of joint production.

Unused empty space in the horizontal tail gives designers some room to maneuver when looking for extra fuel capacity in the future. All versions currently planned, including the ultra-long range -100 will use the existing fuel tanks in the wing. The short bodied aircraft will be capable of flying up to 8,600nm without needing to extend the tanks beyond the wing-fold line.

The 777-200 wing and engine configuration will remain unchanged for both the ultra-long range 777-100 and stretched 777-300. The structure, however, will be "beefed-up" to take the heavier takeoff weights.

and medium-range international routes such as New York to San Francisco or London to New York. Heavier -200s are being built to fly longer range B-market international routes between 5,000 and 8,000 miles (about 8,000 to 12,000km). These include London to Los Angeles and Tokyo to Sydney.

The A- and B-market 777-200s are externally identical. The standard -200, which has a maximum takeoff weight of 506,000 pounds (230,000kg), can fly 4,350 miles (7,010km). Successive A-market aircraft will have additional optional maximum weights of 515,000 pounds (233,600kg) and 535,000 pounds (243,000kg). This allows the aircraft to expand the A-market envelope and cruise for 4,670 miles (7,510km) or 5,330 miles (8,050km), respectively.

The B-market aircraft is structurally heavier to take the larger fuel load of the longer range option. In its basic form, the B is capable of a higher take-off weight of 580,000 pounds (263,090kg) with options of 590,000 pounds (267,60kg), or 632,500 pounds (286,900kg). This latter weight allows the long-range B-market 777 to fly 328 passengers up to 8,320 miles (13,390km).

Airlines such as Cathay Pacific and Korean had also shown interest in a stretched version that Boeing dubbed the 777-300X. This was formally revealed at the 1995 Paris Air Show when Boeing announced "commitments" from four airlines. All Nippon, Cathay Pacific, Korean, and Thai ordered a combined total of 31 -300Xs—twenty of which were new orders and the balance were either confirmations or conversions of earlier -200 orders.

The stretched 777-300 is a huge aircraft aimed at medium range, high-density routes. At 242.3 feet (73.8m) in length, it will be 11 feet (3.4m) longer than the 747 and just 5 feet (1.5m) shorter than the Lockheed C-5 Galaxy. The 777-300 will be the world's third longest aircraft after the Galaxy and the enormous Ukrainian-made Antonov An-225 (a six-engined stretched version of the An-124, which

The 777-200 is fitted with four main exits on each side. The stretched 777-300 will feature an additional Type A door and emergency slide over the wing. The new center body section could also be used for the -100, which will be slightly longer than the 767-300 if built.

transported the 777 engines). To extend the fuselage, a 10-frame plug (17.5 feet or 5.3m) will be inserted forward of the wing while a 9-frame plug (15.75 feet or 4.8m) will be added to the aft fuselage.

The -300 will seat 368 passengers in a typical three-class arrangement, or 451 in a two-class layout. In an all-economy layout, the aircraft could seat as many as 550. It will be used as a 747-100 and -200 replacement on routes up to 6,510 miles (10,500km),

such as San Francisco to Tokyo. The twin-engined economics of the 777-300 mean that it will burn one-third less fuel and will have 40 percent lower maintenance costs than older 747s. The overall result is an operating cost one-third below that of the

With sales exceeding the 200 mark by the mid-1990s, the future looks bright for the 777.

The constant cross-section and inherent growth capability of the new technology powerplants provide ample opportunity for the development of new versions.

747-100/200, or roughly equivalent to the 747-400. The first -300 is expected to be delivered to Cathay Pacific in May 1998, followed by deliveries to All Nippon, Korean, and Thai the same year.

The beefed-up wing structure and undercarriage of the -300 provides the launch platform for yet another version of the 777, the ultra-long range -100X. This "customer-driven" concept basically trades aircraft weight for fuel and would give the "shrink" as it is known within Boeing, the capability to carry 250 passengers up to 10,000 miles (16,100km). One study suggests the aircraft could be shrunk by removing around 10 fuselage frames (17.5 feet or 5.3m) giving it an overall length of just over 190 feet (58m), or just 14 feet (4.2m) longer than the 767-300, the largest version of the long-range twin.

Development of the -100X version will open up the possibility of new nonstop routes that are beyond the range of even the 747-400. These include sectors such as Hong Kong to New York, Dallas to Tokyo, and Singapore to Los Angeles. As with the -300, most of the interest in the -100X is from the Asian-Pacific region airlines like Cathay and Singapore. American Airlines, one of the few early "Working Together" airlines yet to buy the 777, is looking closely at the aircraft as part of its long-term strategy to expand into the Asia-Pacific region. Boeing hopes it can have the first -100X in service by May 1999.

The -100X will be Boeing's main competitor to the long-range Airbus A340-8000 and effectively completes the company's family plan. This may be further supplemented in the future with a long-range version of the 777-300, though this will require some changes, such as the probable use of fuel tanks built into the horizontal tail.

For the moment, the 777 family is well positioned to lead Boeing's attack on the 200- to 400-seat market. This is expected to be worth almost $400 billion between the mid-1990s and 2015, and makes up around 40 percent of an estimated total new-jet market worth almost $1 trillion over the same period.

APPENDIX

OPERATIONAL STATISTICS

777 PROGRAM MILESTONES

	777-200	777-300
Launch	October 29, 1990	June, 1995
Start Major Assembly	January 21, 1993	March, 1997
Rollout	April 9, 1994	August, 1997
First Flight	June 12, 1994	October, 1997
FAA Certification	April 19, 1995	May, 1998
First Delivery	May 15, 1995	May, 1998

(no firm date for the proposed 777-100 is available)

ORDERBOOK

AIRLINE	FIRM	OPTION	
United Airlines	34	34	
All Nippon Airlines	28*	12*	(10 firm/5 option -300)
Euralair	2	0	
Thai Airways Int'l	14*	0	(includes 8 -300s)
British Airways	15	15	
Lauda Air	4	0	
Japan Airlines	15*	10	(includes 5 -300s)
Cathay Pacific	11*	11	(includes 7 -300s)
Emirates	7	7	
ILFC	6	2	
China Southern	6	0	
Continental Airlines	5	5	
Japan Air System	7	0	
Korean Air Lines	12*	8	(includes 8 -300s)
Saudia	23	0	
Egyptair	3	0	
South African Airways	4	3	
Singapore Airlines	28	33	
All Nippon Airlines	6	10	

(listed by order, or intention to order sequence as of November 14, 1995)

DIMENSIONS

	777-200	777-300
Length	209ft 1in (63.7m)	242ft 4in (73.8m)
Wingspan	199ft 11in (60.9m)	199ft 11in (60.9m)
Tail Height	60ft 9in (18.5m)	60ft 9in (18.5m)
Fuselage		
Exterior Diameter	20ft 4in (6.19m)	20ft 4in (6.19m)
Interior Diameter	9ft 3in (5.86m)	19ft 3in (5.86m)

CARGO CAPACITY

Containers	32 LD-3 containers	20 LD-3 containers plus 8 pallets 96in x 125in.
Bulk-Loaded Cargo	600cu ft (17 cu m)	600cu ft (17 cu m)
Total Volume	5, 656cu ft (160.16cu m)	7, 080cu ft (212.4cu m)

MAX TAKEOFF WEIGHT

Initial Models	506,000lb (299,520kg)	660,000lb (299,370kg)
	515,000lb (233,600kg)	
	535,000lb (242,680kg)	
Increased Gross Weight Models	580,000lb (263,090kg)	N/A
	590,000lb (267,620kg)	
	632,500lb (268,900kg)	

RANGE

Initial Models	4,350mi (7,010km)	6,550mi (10,550km)
	6,550mi (10,550km)	
	4,670mi (7,510km)	
	5,330mi (8,580km)	
Increased Gross Weight Models	6,860mi (11,040km)	N/A
	7,160mi (11,040km)	
	8,320mi (13,390km)	

FUEL CAPACITY

	31,000gal (117,345L)	Not available
	45,220 gal (171,171L)	
	44,700gal (169,200L)	

ENGINES

	GE90-75, -76, -85, -92	GE90-92
	PW4074, 4077, 4084, 4090	PW4098
	RR Trent 877, 884, 890	Trent 890

SEATING

Three-class	305-328	368-394
Two-class	375-400	451-479
All economy	418-440	up to 550

Variation in seating depends on the airline's choice of 9- or 10-abreast seating in economy class, and seven or eight abreast in business class.

INDEX